How to become a Crocodile in a Lizard's World

How to become a Crocodile in a Lizard's World

Kent Hodge

Outasight Enterprises

National Library of Australia
Card Number and ISBN 0 9587188 4 9

Published by Outasight Enterprises

P.O. Box 1218
MUDGEERABA QLD 4213 AUSTRALIA
Ph: 0412 151 639

P.O. Box 6242
BRENTWOOD CM14 5FT
UNITED KINGDOM

E-mail:
editor@outasightenterprises.com
Visit our website on:
www.outasightenterprises.com

Manuscripts are always welcomed from prospective
authors of motivational/inspirational material.
Please request a Submissions Guideline
from the Editor.

PRINTED IN AUSTRALIA

This book is dedicated to
Benson Idahosa:

A man who altered the destiny
of Africa, impacted millions
of lives around the globe and
whom my wife and I had
the privilege of working with
closely for 13 years.

Contents

Preface

Working in Africa, my wife and I have both been training leaders for the past 15 years. During that time we have gathered, sponsored, trained and then released over 7,000 leaders. Many people from Africa and other nations around the world have stood with us to help us to achieve this goal. In that period of time, new leaders have gone to almost every nation on the African continent and to some 50 other nations around the world. Together they are directly impacting millions of lives.

Training leaders was the vision of my mentor Benson Idahosa. He once said, *'A lizard in Africa cannot be a crocodile in America'*. Escaping to another place will not change who you are. The principles of life, relationships and success work when they are applied, no matter where you live or what your occupation is.

Benson Idahosa founded over 100 schools for primary and secondary education. He founded two hospitals and a government accredited university. He also founded a training institution for the leaders of tomorrow, over which my wife and I were given the responsibility as directors. Since becoming the leaders of the college, the institute has grown to a population of 1,600 trainee leaders from 26 nations of Africa and Europe.

Training leaders is turning lizards into crocodiles – timid beginners into confident achievers. We have seen the principles work in so many lives. It is now your turn. Take the words of this book and apply them to your own life and surroundings. You will see your life develop as you learn to take on new challenges and win. You will make winning your habit.

CHAPTER 1

Your Best Asset: Your Right of Choice

*S*omething you will always have is choice. It is the way you have been created. You may not always be able to choose your circumstances or surroundings, but you can choose your attitude and response. No one and no situation can take your freedom of choice away from you.

So often, we react to circumstances. We feel we are pinned in and we have no choice. Instead of using our choice, we submit to circumstances as if they were our masters. The slave to circumstances reacts to their problems and just compounds them. However, the person in control chooses their action. They take control. They are not futile reactors. They are people of action. They plan their action. They plot their course, determine their preferred course, and take it.

> **You may not be able to determine the circumstances around you but you can determine how you will respond to them.**

In Africa we train leaders who serve in over one hundred nations around the world. Once several years ago, I had a desire to expand the enrolment of students in the institution. I went to my boss, who had founded the institute, and explained to him the vision and what was required to facilitate it. After listening to me intently for over an hour he said, *'It is a good thing to do. Go ahead and do it. Meanwhile, would you like a cup of tea?'*

Well, of course, I did not want a cup of tea – I wanted his help. I was angry.

Over the years, I have been very thankful for that interaction and for many others like it that followed. My mentor taught me to respond the right way. I had a choice. I could blame his lack of help for not accomplishing our vision or I could decide that he was right – that I was able to go ahead and do it, without him always carrying me.

The cup of tea was the right thing to have at that time. He threw in a meal as well. I took it, though I was not in the mood to enjoy it. It wasn't what I wanted. I wanted tangible help immediately, not a mere assurance that I had what it took to get me through the task. But the man was right. I succeeded in the task ahead and above all, I learnt that no matter what was ahead of me, I could accomplish it.

You can choose what is important in life. You can have priorities. You may not be able to achieve everything you want at once, but you can choose which things are most important to you at that time. You can choose to do what's right. It might not always be easy. Circumstances may make it tough. However, you are not the slave of circum-stances. You can choose to love. You can choose to believe and you can choose to be trustworthy.

You can choose how you think. You can think on good things or you can think on harmful things. You can think positively or negatively. Sometimes it may seem hard to make that choice. Sometimes you have to break old habits, especially with your thinking patterns. You may have to work hard to break bad habits and train yourself in good habits. But it is worth it. Lasting success does not come accidentally. If you have trained yourself in what are called *'the bad times'*; you will be prepared in your character to handle *'the good times'*. Good success needs good character. If you concentrate on training your character you will make the right choices at the critical times of life.

> **Good life
> comes from making
> good choices
> at the
> critical times.**

You need character to go on; to go through the tough spots. Personality or the *'gift of the gab'* can get you quick success, but only character can bring you good, lasting success. It takes time.

> **A building built well
> is a building built strong.
> The same principle
> applies to your life.**

You can choose whom you relate with. If you want to achieve something big, relate with people who have done at least twice what you want to do. They will give you the right tips. Don't learn from those who have never achieved the goals you are aiming for. Don't ask a cook how to fix a motorcar. You can choose to learn from others.

> ## Who you mix with determines the advice you will build your life on.

Some people are successful in one realm, but not in other realms. In business, take advice from those who have achieved what you want to achieve. In your marriage and family affairs, take advice from people who have succeeded in that field. Everyone has opinions, but it is what works that matters. Follow what works. To be successful you must relate to successful people. You will then be better equipped to relate to people who are unsuccessful and to help them become successful. If you want someone successful to relate to you, find others that you can also help.

You can choose not to blame others. While you blame others, you are failing to discover what you can do about the situation. Blaming others makes you a slave to the circumstances. It is a reaction. It doesn't fix anything. You need to ask, *'What can I do to help ensure that this same outcome does not occur again?'* The man who blames his wife will not grow in love and patience. The boss who blames his employee will not learn to be a good manager of people and departments. The person that blames the horoscope will not learn that the things that happen to him are the result of his choices.

Someone once said, *'You are what you are today, because that is what you chose to be'*. It is not because of what someone else has done to you. The same things have happened to other people, but it didn't stop them. They didn't use it as an excuse.

> ## Don't look for excuses to fail, look for ways to succeed.

When you have a problem, you can choose not to go into denial. You can choose not to justify yourself. When you admit a problem exists, you stand the best chance of doing something positive about it. It is then that you have a choice that didn't exist before. You can choose what positive action you can take to fix the problem.

> **The first step in getting out of your problem is to admit that it exists.**

Don't blame the market. Plan a new strategy. Don't get bitter about those who let you down. If someone lets you down, don't let yourself down. There is nobody in the world who has been exempt from market force or who has not been let down by others. You can choose not to be bitter. You can choose to be free of the shackles of anger. You can choose to identify better people whom you can work with next time. There are many good people in the world today. If you invest trust and hope in others, you will find that the best will be drawn out of them. You can choose the way you relate with others. Instead of bullying people into doing what you want, you can teach them with dignity. If someone does what you want because you force them, it is not love. However, if they do something good because they choose to, that is love.

So there are many choices that you and only you have control over. You are today what you have chosen to be. Nobody else can choose your attitudes. Your attitudes determine your behaviour and your behaviour determines your results in the area of relationships and in the results you will see in your life.

> **The only thing that is needed is maturity. You have every other gift within you.**

It is your choice. You can respond to circumstances by growing. You have to stretch. Do you

want successful people to do it for you or do you
want to become successful like them?

CHAPTER 2

Prioritize
Your
Success

*J*n what areas of your life do you want to succeed? You will eventually obtain what you go after and you will hit what you are aiming at. What then are you aiming at? Have you worked out in your heart what real success is? Do you really know what you want? Do you know what is most important to you? Have you thought about it, or are you just following one impulse after another? Do you set your goals on your own or are others involved in your equation? Are your goals your own or are they shared with others?

Some people have a very shallow idea of success. What I mean by shallow is that their ideas have not been well thought out. This is where you have to start making priorities. You cannot succeed at everything. You cannot be a fireman, a policeman and an airline pilot all at once. You have to decide what is most important for you and go for that.

Do you discuss and incorporate other people's aspirations into your goals? You can only succeed as those around you do. You are not an independent island. Does your success include the success of your associates? Does your success include the success of your family?

> ### Success on its own is not success.
> ### It must be 'our success' rather than 'my success'.

When people set their goals for financial success, they may not have really thought out the reason why they do that. Why do you want to succeed financially? Is it so that you can have what the next-door neighbour has? Do you want to be better than other people are? Is that what success means to you? If it is, you may be sacrificing very important parts of your life – namely relationships.

Is succeeding at relationships one of your goals? How high a priority is succeeding in your relationship with your spouse, your children and your work colleagues?

Have you defined what success is for you? If you are married, have you sat down together with your spouse and defined together what success is for both of you? It is wonderful to be able to do that with your spouse.

> ### Head somewhere together as a team.
> ### Have a strong agreement and work hard
> ### together in partnership.

Success is being able to work together with others. Success is having a joint vision with shared accomplishments. Not *'I did it my way'*, but *'we did it the right way'.*

If your goals are yours alone then you may end up treading on the people around you to achieve them. Some of these people may be your close friends, even your children or spouse. If your goals are joint goals then you will move forward together. You don't have to tread on others, because you have sincerely and honestly incorporated their values and desires in your joint goals.

> **When setting goals,**
> **incorporate the values of others**
> **into your goals.**

You don't want to arrive at your goal on your own. That would lead to a lonely existence and one that may not be worth arriving at. When you learn to incorporate the values of others in your goal setting then you will inevitably arrive together at the same destination.

> **This is the best type of success.**
> **Success with others,**
> **not success at the cost of others.**

Someone I know said that prosperous means *'prosper us'*. True prosperity is shared with others. Our goals can be established with the view of including others.

When we put financial success or career success as the first priority then it is possible that we will leave others behind. We can get such a single focus on one thing that we forget how others are feeling and forget the needs of the ones we love the most.

A good priority for success may be your relationships. To succeed with your spouse is a proof of success in your own heart. If you cannot succeed in your own house then what do you have to 'sell'?

> ### If your 'product' is exportable, then surely it should work at home.

What about your children? If success means that the video player, video games or behaviour modifying drugs become your children's baby sitter, then your success belongs only to you and not to them. For children to succeed, they need meaningful relationships with their parents. You must become interested in their goals. You must stand beside them each day to move them towards their full potential with love, care and discipline.

> ### Success is good when it is shared success

It is good when your success includes the goal of establishing and maintaining good relationships with those around you. Life is boring when you take your own path without including anyone else.

> ### When you succeed at relationships, you have a purpose for your financial success.

Your purpose is to share. It is to lift up others. That is what gives money its value. It can help others when it is used in the right way.

When it comes to priorities, which one would you sacrifice first – a relationship or a sale? If your foundation is right and you put first things first, life has a purpose beyond what you can get out of it. That purpose is other people.

Life is not about what you can get out of it, but what you can put into it. That is where the joy is. That is where the sense of accomplishment and value is. When you value others, you will learn to value yourself.

Many people have a wrong concept of leadership. They feel that it is a time for self-fulfilment. But a leader serves the interests of others, not of him or herself.

Over the years, we have lived in a few temporary houses. In one place, my wife and I planted a couple of avocado seeds. It takes seven years for an avocado seed to grow into a tree that bares fruit. People thought us very strange for planting a tree from which we would never eat the fruit. Our joy though was that others would eat the fruit.

That is success. Your priorities include others. You may not enjoy the full benefit of what you are building now but you have foresight. You know that generations ahead will have the foundation for a prosperous future. Successful people think of the future of others.

CHAPTER 3

Be
Teachable

*A*s a youth, I would often go with my parents to our weekend farm. My father worked in the city, but he tried to make the farm work as well. It was a hobby and a retreat, but he also tried to make it succeed financially as a farm.

I remember helping my father to put up the new electric fencing system. We rammed poles into the ground and erected miles of new fencing with my other brothers. When the cattle saw the fencing for the first time, they didn't know what to make of it. I assume they wondered whether we were serious, expecting such thin strands of wire to hold them back. So they approached with caution, one at a time.

The first beast slowly touched the wire and then jumped back with a big jolt. She then took off, running through a mountainside paddock. But that display was not enough for the rest of the herd. The next cow approached carefully. After touching the fence gently, she followed the same procedure as the first and off she went. Still the others followed. One after another, each cow had to experience the new fence for themselves.

> ## Cows are not able to learn from the experience of others.

They know not to get stuck in the mud at water holes, not because they saw a dead cow there before, but because they have almost died there themselves. As humans though, we should learn from the experience of others.

> ## It is much better
> ## if we can learn from
> ## the experience of others.

Biographies can help in this way. Unfortunately, many biographies do not paint the picture of the negative side of a person's life. We are often led to think that they were born to success, but the truth is that they struggled with the same failings in life that each of us does.

When we set out to learn from other people's mistakes or victories, the first step is that we need to be good observers. Those who are too quick to voice abroad their own opinions on a matter are not always good observers.

Someone I know advised me that we should *'open our ears, open our eyes and shut our mouth'*. This is especially important when you are around someone that is more experienced than you are. That is an excellent opportunity to learn. Observing others is not a common skill. Often people are too busy thinking about how they look in the eyes of others rather than looking.

> **Good communication skills are essential
> to success in life.**

People who are skilled observers are skilled communicators. Some people go through each day filled with their own problems, never seeing, never hearing what is going on in the lives of others.

> **90% of communication is listening.**

Only 10% is your reply. Some don't listen at all, but spend the whole time the other person is talking thinking of what they will say as soon as they get their next chance.

> **Can you see a matter from the other
> person's perspective?**

Can you understand *'where the other person is coming from'*? Are you really listening? Or do you hear and see everything through your own perspective, values, experiences and culture?

This doesn't mean that there is no objective truth. It doesn't mean that reality is in the eye of the beholder, that the universe is an infinite set of individual subjective experiences. What it does mean is that before you can bring someone to an objective reality, you must first understand how they think and why they are the way they are.

> **It takes a compassionate and
> empathetic heart to patiently understand
> other people.**

The key point in this chapter is *'learn'*. If you

ever want to get ahead, don't ever think you know it all. If you have tried something ten times and it hasn't worked, then why try it again the same way. Learn and do it differently the next time, until you get it right. There is a right way. Find it.

A good way to learn is to learn from others. This takes humility. Other people are rough diamonds with many rough edges that offend. If you can look past those and stick with that person, long enough to learn from them, you can gain invaluable insight and make good progress in life.

How many times did Thomas Edison get the light bulb wrong before he got it right? Time after time he tried different substances, but they would not contain light without burning. He didn't give up. Each time he tried again, but not the same way as before. He thought about a new approach. He finally got it right. He didn't give up until he got it right.

> ## When we stop learning, we stop growing.

In a neighbourhood in Africa where I lived for several years, the town water supply was totally ineffective. Eventually we had to sink a 200-ft deep bore in order to obtain sufficient water for everybody's needs. At that depth, there was an overwhelming supply of water.

On ground level, many people went to great trouble to get water. However, there was more than enough water for everybody just under their feet.

> ## The difference between lack and sufficiency is knowledge.

There is more than enough available. We just need the knowledge to access it. Knowledge unlocks whole new ways of doing things. So, be teachable.

> ## Never say, 'It can't be done'.

Learn from those who have done it. A valuable team member is one who listens. I would rather have a listener working with me than one who has all the formal qualifications.

When I left college, after studying business, I thought I was ready for the corporate world. In my first job, I found out that I didn't even have the basic skill of how to follow instructions. I had a boss whom I thought was a bit rude. She threw work back in my face repeatedly until I did it exactly the way she wanted. I didn't like the way she treated me, but I did learn to listen.

When passing messages from one team member to another I have found one thing that must be avoided: *'Chinese whispers'*. Whenever I send someone with a message, I always ask him or her to repeat the message to me first. I make sure they have it right.

If you have a team member to whom you can say *'do A, B, and C'*, and they do A, B, and C, they are valuable. However, there are many who don't listen and then go away and do E, F and G.

When you do as you are asked, then qualifications are not nearly as important.

> ## The world is looking for listeners.

If you are a listener and if you are teachable, you are valuable. This is the most important thing, for you can train anyone to be qualified but not everyone will listen.

CHAPTER 4

Go Forward

*L*ife is like driving a car. When you are driving, you spend most of your time looking forward.

Stay focused on your destination.

You don't drive looking in your rear vision mirror. If you are on a tractor and you are ploughing a field, the only way to plough a straight line is to keep your eyes fixed on a position in front of you. You fix your eyes on the point of your destination. That is your reference point.

If you try to evaluate whether you are driving in a straight line by looking down at the ground you are ploughing, you cannot plough straight. You must be focused ahead of yourself.

In life, you must have a vision.

This vision becomes your focus. It keeps you in a straight line. It makes sure you are acting with proper purpose each day.

Focusing on your vision informs you of the things that need to be accomplished each day. So while you are focused ahead you are very much aware of the details that you are attending to at any moment.

> ### A visionary is not someone who has his head in the clouds.
> ### They pay attention to detail.

They know that by doing it right, by paying close attention to details, it will get them closer to their goal. To be a success you need to focus on two points. One is a clear picture of your goals. The other is a work ethic that does not shy away from the nitty-gritty details of getting each task along the way, accomplished on schedule.

A goal is a large task. It can look daunting. You will never realise your dreams unless you learn to break them down into smaller pieces and achieve one step at a time. Start with your destination in mind. Then determine each step that must be accomplished for you to arrive at the destination. That is how you achieve success. Someone said, *'You divide to conquer'*.

> ### Successful people are both visionary and detail managers.

You must be both to go forward. You must know where you are going and what you will have to do to get there. It has been said that *'the devil is in the details'*. There have been many great ideas that failed on lift off because people have not hammered out the details.

The past stops many people from going forward. For some, it is a good past. You think on successes you have had and lose focus on a new and better destination. This is where *'good becomes the enemy of better'*.

Don't drive with your gaze fixed on the rear vision mirror.

Forget the things that are behind you and go forward.

Our cars nevertheless have rear vision mirrors for a purpose. You do need to refer to the things behind you but you don't focus on them. Past experiences can teach you and they are definitely reference points for future decisions. But that is all.

> **Learn lessons from the past;
> work hard in the present and focus
> on the future.**

Focusing on the future is the only way to make sure that your work in the present is spent on the right things and that you are not wasting your efforts.

In our past we may have had bad experiences. These can prevent us from going forward. Many people have their focus on past bad experiences. This can become a mental habit. It is a habit that must be broken, sometimes by diligent and determined effort.

Have you heard the story about the dog that was tied up for months in one place? It would run until it came to the end of its chain, where it would be brought to a sudden and painful holt. When the dog was finally let loose, for a while it didn't believe it. It still behaved as though it was tied up and limited to its previous domain. Experience had taught the dog its limitations.

Some people live like that. Their past limitations become their belief patterns for what they can do in the future. They limit themselves by focusing on past failures. The chain only exists if they focus on it.

People may have offended you. These past experiences can affect the way you treat the people the next time you meet. Even if you meet different people, your behaviour towards them can be effected by experiences you have had from others in the past. You may stereotype and classify people by your past experiences with others. Sometimes you carry the memory of bitter experiences that become chains around your neck. You focus on hurts from people you have loved, or even hurts from people you have never met before.

> **For you to go forward you must let the past go.**

You must forget the rudeness of people you come in contact with each day. They often don't mean anything personal towards you. They are usually just responding to their own frustrations in life. To go forward you must put all these things behind you.

> **Those who travel forward carry little baggage.**

The faster you want to go forward, the less baggage you must carry. You must travel light. Forget the things that are behind you. They are too heavy to carry. Learn to forgive. You can't afford not to. You have achieved in the past. Expect greater achievements in the future.

Somebody once asked a friend of mine, *'What is the greatest achievement you have ever had?'* He answered, *'My next one'.*

CHAPTER 5

Be Organised

*I*f you want to keep customers, you need to deliver what you promise. Your product or service must be consistent in quality. People need to know what they can expect from you. They must have the confidence that what they expect is what they are going to get. If you say you will deliver at a certain time, it must be consistent with what you have said. If you promise a certain quality then you must deliver repeatedly.

The same principle applies to the way you share your vision. If you are not clear in your own mind about what you are doing, then you cannot expect other people to catch your vision.

> **Two things that are essential in any enterprise are vision and communication.**

Do you know what your product or service is? Are you very clear about what you are doing? Do you know what people need? Are you able to provide that?

You are not ready to grow and expand until you have firstly identified people's need. Then you must be organised in such a way as to meet those needs. Once you have done that, you must communicate your vision very clearly to others. Be clear. Be organised in your thinking and presentation. People must know what you are talking about.

Once you have delivered your vision, you must fulfil the commitments you have made. This is what gives your vision reality and integrity. People know that they can trust you and that you don't have your head in the clouds.

The same goes for your family. When you communicate something to your spouse or your children they need to know that you mean it. They need to know that you have a vision for them and that you have a plan in place to fulfil what you have said. You must also have the commitment to stick with the plan until it produces the results you desire. However, if you are disorganised, you will frustrate your family, your friends and your market.

Organisation gives you three things. Organisation will give you clarity of vision, precise communication and reality. Make sure you back up your great ideas with consistent action.

Someone once said, *'Unction without action is auctioned'*. Unction is an idea. Unless you act on it, you lose it.

'Use it or lose it'.
Ideas are for acting on.

Don't live in emergency mode. Some people don't work on something until the last possible minute. They are always in catch up mode. If you do that, no one will catch your vision.

> **You must think and then act ahead of time.**

Ask yourself, *'What will I have to do next month? What can I do now in preparation for what must be fulfilled next month?'* Act ahead of time. Prepare ahead of time. Don't do things the day they are needed. Begin well in advance.

When you are organised, you have time to do extra. You have time to dream and to think about innovations and improvements, because you have already done the essential things.

There are two areas of activity. Firstly, those things that are essential. These are the basic day-to-day tasks that must be done for you to get from point A to point B. You should anticipate as many of these as possible and get them out of the way ahead of time.

This then gives you time for the second vital area of activity. This is lateral thinking, dreaming and implementing innovations. This is not the emergency field of operation. It is the planning side. Many people do not function in this area because they are too busy running around in emergency mode. They are unorganised.

When you come to lateral thinking, you are identifying your bottlenecks and investigating ways of removing them.

> **Growth occurs when you identify
> and remove bottlenecks.**

Water only flows out of a bottle as fast as the neck allows, no matter the capacity of the bottle. *'A chain is only as strong as its weakest link'*. *'A fleet is only as fast as its slowest ship'*. Find out which of the ships is the slowest and discover and implement ways of making it faster. This is how you grow. It doesn't happen by accident. Look for the weakest link – strengthen it.

It might be difficult to find a way of removing the bottleneck, or of making that ship faster. But that is the factor that you must be working on. You have now identified the area of concern – where the shoe is rubbing the foot. You are not going to grow until you solve that problem.

Only those people who do this will grow. Those who function in catch up mode will never have the time to concentrate on important innovations.

You grow by not neglecting the weakest member.

This might not be obvious to everyone. Usually we give most attention to the strongest member. But that is not always right. You should not concentrate on a few strong people. No enterprise can make a lasting impact based only upon heroes.

You must build the team. You do this by building up the weakest members. Make the team strong. When a group is walking in the countryside, you are only going to walk as fast as the slowest person does. So, seek to improve the skills of everyone on the team. Everyone is important. Don't fall for the temptation of relying on a few. Build the talents and skills of everyone around you.

Growth always requires change.

In the college I direct we had a class that held 400 people. It wouldn't hold any more. That was our bottleneck. The student's desks had a tabletop width of two feet. I called a carpenter in to cut six inches off the width of all the tables. One and a half feet is plenty for a student's books. No book is two feet in height. So with that minor adjustment we could now fit 500 students in the class. Later we had a much bigger class.

To remove bottlenecks we must be ready to sacrifice some traditions. You may have to do something that will upset people. You shouldn't be out to upset people and you should try to help people understand, but you cannot sacrifice progress just because someone doesn't like change.

You cannot grow unless you identify the areas that need to be changed and find a way of doing it. This requires leadership. A leader can see what needs to be changed and is willing to make a change. When a person builds their own establishment and protects it, then they are no longer fit to be the leader. Someone who is willing to make changes must take their place. The work must go on.

> ## A leader makes changes.

But not change for change sake. You don't change something that is working. You change the slowest ship. You have to hit the right target.

We had a dining room that could only cater for 300 students. However, we had to cater for 600 at a time. We had turned the dining hall into another boarding hostel and used the main class for catering after the lectures had finished.

People didn't like this because they thought we shouldn't eat on class tables. So we put tablecloths down before eating.

The *'big issue'* though was the line up for the meals. The head cook always used one queue and it was too slow for 600 people. I suggested that she should use two queues, but she said she could not do that. She was convinced that I didn't understand why she had to use one queue and she was right, I could not understand. If we had used two queues then all the students could have finished their meal within 45 minutes. I still don't understand why we couldn't do that. Change was too hard for her to comprehend.

Organisation helps you to get the mundane out of the way so you can implement innovation. It is not that the mundane is unimportant. Mundane exercises are very important. But the more time you set aside for innovative thought, the greater the growth.

A leader is willing to change, even those things that he has previously implemented himself. If you are not ready to change you are not qualified to lead a group forward towards growth and a successful future.

> **You must adapt to your environment.**

Adaptation is not random change. It is intelligent design. You consider how to solve problems while also considering the feelings of other people and listening to their ideas. Creation has design. It is organised. If your bodily functions were not organised and synchronised, they would not work in harmony. You would not be alive.

If a part of your body is sick, that is the part that gets attention. When you treat your work and your team like that, you will grow.

For you to succeed you need to be organised. When you face daily tasks ahead of time and then identify and cut out bottlenecks one at a time, growth is inevitable. Organise yourself to address those things each day that are necessary.

> **Don't beat the air. Strike the target.**
> **That is organisation.**

CHAPTER 6

Work

*M*any people want a bigger slice of the cake. However, unless the cake is bigger, not everyone can get a bigger slice. So instead of demanding your rights you can endeavour to increase the size of the cake.

> **Increased output
> leads to
> increased income.**

There are no short cuts here. It's not the complainers that get ahead. Instead of wasting precious energy complaining, you can spend it planning. Working is the best way to increase productivity. Increasing productivity increases income.

Work needs to be diligent and it needs to be planned. A blunt axe takes a long time to fell a tree. Sharpen the axe and the job is easier. Proper planning makes work more effective. Increase your output for any given unit of effort.

> ### Prayerful preparation prevents poor performance.

Now is the time to work hard, not later. Don't wait for when things are better or circumstances are more conducive. There are many reasons to put off work until later. That habit however will stop you from succeeding.

> ### A successful person has defeated the procrastination virus.

You must be able to make decisions to succeed. Only those who take personal responsibility for their decisions and are not afraid to make them can get ahead. Those who have no courage to decide will never change anything.

A successful person is not a workaholic, but is always producing something. Whether it is in relationships, in rest or in the office, they are productive. In rest, they rebuild their life. Rest is productive.

> ### Make work your habit and lifestyle. Use your time productively.

The person who refuses to work will die disappointed. They will never know if they could have realised their vision. They are frustrated in life. They have desires and visions that are never fulfilled and skills that are never fully developed and used.

You are born with certain skills, but it takes work to maximise their usefulness. Think of Olympians, how much they train – how they set their sights on a goal and force themselves to put in the training necessary to achieve it. That is what it will take you to be a success.

You must work at it like an Olympian. Unless an Olympian works hard at training and watches their diet they cannot and will not win a medal. The Olympian must have discipline.

> **Vision without discipline is untapped potential. It is unharnessed power.**

People who succeed by chance usually lose what they have very quickly. *'Easy come, easy go'.* These are those who are always waiting for their lucky break. They refuse to work in order to carve out their future.

We all have good breaks, but you have to be ready to take full advantage of them when they come.

Lottery winners often find themselves in their original condition not long after their windfall. Why? Because that is who they are. They are poor in character. Therefore, their state in life always gravitates back to their character.

On the other hand, if someone is a millionaire in their character, no matter how many times they fall, they will rise again. No matter what circumstances they find themselves in they will always rise to the top. Why? Because that is their character. That is who they are.

> **Work must be your character.**

When you work you pay the price. You appreciate the fruits of your labour because of the effort you have expended. You then become a good manager. Success becomes a habit, not an occasional accident.

You can make success a habit.

You can make anything a habit. Some habits are easier to form than others. The good ones take some pain. But it is good pain because you know you are going to win.

You may become tired when sowing a field but you know you are going to reap a harvest. You take the pain with joy. When success is a habit, you expect it. You are conditioned for it. You put in the work that is naturally required.

When people are time orientated, they grow tired easily. They start work at a certain time and they finish at a certain time. They are clock-watchers. Work for them is slavery. Life doesn't start until the clock reaches a certain time. These people often hate Mondays, because it means a whole week of clock watching is ahead.

Successful people are task orientated.

They think in terms of tasks not time. They come to work to achieve certain goals. Work is a joy because they know they are achieving something that is worthwhile. These people don't work for a pay packet at the end of the week. They work because they are achieving something that is worth their time and effort. Their life has a sense of value because their work has purpose.

Work is a privilege, not a duty.

Work gives you value because you can achieve something that is helpful to others. Lazy people don't value their time and have a lower value of themselves. Work can change the way we value ourselves.

Since you spend so much time each day of your lives at work, it is very important that you have a correct perspective on it. Why waste your life in doing something you hate? It doesn't make sense. Work requires a valid motive, a good plan and diligent effort.

Look at old people. Many who retire and have no hobby or purpose don't live long. Purposeful work gives you life. It causes you to live longer. Work is a good thing. If everything were done for you, you would have no reason to exist.

It is a good thing that you have to stand up, roll up our sleeves. Be determined not to give up until you have carved out a living for your family by working. It is a privilege. It gives you respect and gives your life meaning.

Some people say, *'I'll try for a while, but if this doesn't work or if the pain is too great I'll give up'*. If you say that, then you want to win without fighting. That is not what life is about. Life is for heroes.

> ## Without obstacles, what story of success can you have?

If things go wrong you can't say, *'I tried and it's not fair.'* Stop saying, *'Life isn't fair'*. Worse has happened to others and they got up and went again, and again, and again, and again. If they can do it, so can you.

You have to defeat laziness. Laziness raises its head in many different ways. Excuse making is a favourite camouflage for laziness. Stop making excuses. Look for reasons. When you find the reason that something went wrong, you can do something positive about it. You can change. However, excuses are poor justification for procrastination and laziness.

Don't argue with life. Get up and get going. You can't have it your way all the time. You just have to face facts. Life isn't against you. Your case is no different to anybody else. No one is picking on you.

Gravity is not against you. It is just a law of nature. Instead of complaining about it, learn to harness it for your favour. Work with the laws of nature. Don't fight them. Use them. They are there to help you.

**Life is not against you.
It is trying to teach you something.**

This is where education is so important. Some people make the same mistakes over and over. Others learn the way the world is made and work with it. The world is there to help you succeed. You have to learn how it works and work with it. The world won't change for you. You must change. You just have to make a decision, *'I am going to win.'*

Turn your excuses to uses.

CHAPTER 7

Study Opens New Doors

*E*ducation is one of the opportunities that can change your future. Knowledge is a key that can unlock doors that you didn't even know existed. If you know how to sharpen an axe you can cut down a tree in a quarter of the time you would do it with a blunt axe.

Some of the people we train in Africa have little education when we start with them. We do not teach literacy as a main part of what we do, but with hundreds of people to teach, we have to teach some of them the basics of literacy before we are able to start on other things.

One student from the nation of Ghana was illiterate when he came to us. After graduation, he went back to his country to work. No one would employ him, but he refused to give up. Now, thousands of Ghanaians would like that very same man to employ them. He has risen to a level where he has helped shape the future of the nation. Standing alongside the president of Ghana, this once uneducated man has influenced the lives of millions for good.

It is not your current state of education that matters, but your hunger for education.

> **If you are hungry to learn you will advance.**

There are so many things you do every day that you could do better. Education turns on a light on the inside of you and shows you something good that you have never seen before.

Opposed to this is the cynical way. *'I have seen it all'* or *'I know it all.'* This is what distinguishes a child from some adults. A child does not know what cannot be done. They approach everything as though it were new. They are forever expecting some new breakthrough in knowledge.

> **Be like a child,
> for they are forever exploring.**

When we stop exploring, we die on the inside. There is so much we have never seen before. One new idea can change so many things. This idea could come at any time. Things can change in five minutes. Never make a major decision when you are discouraged. Wait five more minutes and something good will happen to you. Then wait another five minutes.

> **Education gives you choices.**

When you have skills you can choose which country you will live in and you can choose which job you will take. You have a commodity that other people want. Get educated.

Don't say it is too late. Someone said, *'I will be forty years old when I finish that course'*. How old will you be in three years if you don't do the course? Do the course.

Information is the basis for good decision-making.

Our office building in Africa is five stories high. Our staff cannot run up and down to consult with others every time they are making a decision. With hundreds of decisions being made every day, our staff must have information from other departments that have a bearing on the decisions they make.

Because their decisions need to be informed decisions, we installed an intercom system that allowed for clear communication between the five floors. All day the telephones are ringing between offices, as people are discussing the decisions they are making. It is communication. The right decisions are made.

Information is essential to good decision-making. Always find out the other side of the story first. Get educated.

Don't react to second hand information. Go to the original source and get the full picture.

Find out more. Always talk to people before you make a decision. You need statistics. You need market information. You need information on trends. You need information on every aspect related to what you are doing. You need information, information, and information ... as much as you can get.

Once you have this information, it needs to be organised in such a way to reveal trends. That is why I use graphs and tables. The information is summarised for myself and others to look at and to use. The graphs must relate to factors that I have the power to change.

Have reasons for the decisions you make. Ask those you work with for the reasons they have made decisions. Reasons must be based on information.

Information shows you what happened as a result of certain decisions you made. Now you will know what is likely to happen the next time you make a similar decision. Study your data.

> ### Don't operate on fables. Don't guess.
> ### Get the information.

To have information, you need systems set up that will catch it. You need to start taking statistics. If you are new to the field, ask others who have been there for a while.

We all need education. In our society, education is one thing that is available to all. Everyone has the chance to be educated. No matter what family background you come from you must be educated. Without education, a person's birth status can adversely determine their future.

There was a woman I know, who was born in a Nigerian village. She did not allow her economic situation to adversely determine her future. Her family had no money to educate her. Her father had many wives. She was one of 30 children born to him. What did she matter?

Sons were valued more highly in that family, not education. The sons would work the farms. That was life, from one generation to another. But this young girl valued education. She wanted life to be different.

> **A different life begins with a decision
> backed by commitment.**

So she worked. She rented land and grew crops. She sold them for the money she needed for school fees. She put herself through secondary school, even though her family didn't help her. She valued education. She went out and got it. Now her life and the lives of her children have broken out of the inherited cycle.

Do you value education that much? If you do, you can break out and break through towards a greater future. For all of us, our real life education needs to continue throughout our whole life.

CHAPTER 8

Character: The Way to Long Term Success

*I*f you want a short-term solution to your problems, that can be fairly easy to achieve. You can increase productivity by forcing others to work harder. However, that may not develop in them the respect that is needed for strong teamwork. A strong team is far more productive, but that takes time to develop.

> **You must have
> a long-term approach towards
> building powerful
> partners in business.**

Being patient with people may not achieve quick results in the short-term. You may not get what you want as soon as you want it. This may apply not only in the work place, but also in the home. However, when you treat others with respect, you are laying the proper groundwork for strong relationships that have been built on trust.

A strong business environment is based upon trust. When people can work together as a team, they can be very productive. Powerful creativity is released through people when they know that they are trusted and that they have respect through a delegation of authority. It is a risk to delegate properly, but it shows trust. In the long-term, you are looking for the type of relationship with other people that will bring forth the maximum initiative. When you want everything done your way, you stop other people contributing their own skills towards improving the environment.

> **Dictators are finally impoverished.**
> **Facilitators are enriched**
> **by the skills of other people**
> **around them.**

So your function in life is not so much to govern, but to facilitate. You don't see other people as factors of production, but you see them as whole persons with aspirations, dignity and potential that has been given to them by their creator. You facilitate the growth of others. Through proper communication you value the expression of others and encourage their personal growth in an environment of hope, trust and faith.

> **Once you view people as people and not as tools,**
> **you have set a right foundation**
> **for maximum output.**

You may not get off to a quick start this way. It may be much faster at first to dominate. But by dominating you will only go so far, only as far as you can take it by yourself. To really succeed though, you need to have a sincere interest in others that will allow for a combination of the talents of every person. Every person has something good to offer.

> **You must have a long-term approach to developing character. Good character can never be beaten.**

Another area where we need a long-term view is with the development of our own personal character. Let's say we are made of two parts, personality and character. We can rely on our personality to make a sale. We may call it the *'gift of the gab'*, or *'making an impression'*. Not everyone is confident in this area. Some don't seem to have much personality. Does that mean that if you don't have a lot of personality that you cannot succeed? No. For there is another more important area of your life and that is your character. It takes longer to develop because character grows as you develop good habits. It takes time. You work on one area of your life and then another. In the long run character produces what we may call fruit. I call it fruit because it takes time to develop.

You can be born with a personality, but you have to develop character. So how do you develop character? How do you develop fruit? You don't force the tree to bare fruit. You must provide a suitable environment for the tree and then the fruit will grow naturally. The tree needs the right amount of sunlight, moisture and nutrients in the soil.

> **Healthy relationships with other people help develop your character.**

You might call sunlight your relationships with others. You might call the soil the right kind of food. To develop character you need food. This comes in the form of inspiration and the right form of learning. This involves study, books, tapes, seminars and learning from life's experiences.

You can be happy because something is going well for you or you can be happy because it is the fruit of living right over many years. When you make right decisions over many years, that have a positive impact on people around you, you are building a strong foundation for lasting happiness. Selfish lifestyles erode real happiness.

> **It takes time to develop real deep, lasting and enduring joy.**

Happiness is not based upon our daily experiences. People think that if they could just have this or that they would be happy, or if they could just experience the latest in entertainment. Riches do not make you happy. Promotions do not make you happy. Happiness comes from your character. Character is developed over a long period of deliberately making the right decisions in life.

Happiness is not an experience; it is a fruit of character. You know that fruit takes time to grow. Fruit takes time to develop. And when you have it, it stays, no matter what is going on around you. It is a foundation that cannot be eroded.

> **The way to get good fruit is to do right.**

When you develop the habit of making the right decisions in your daily affairs and relationships you will begin to enjoy life.

Again, this takes time. At first, it may cost you to do right. This is why you cannot be short-term minded when it comes to success. Success is built over time. It is built into your marriage, your children and into your work place environment. When your marriage is going well, you have joy.

When your children are growing up well and can look life in the eyes and win, you have joy. This is what everybody desires. It makes life worth living. It makes your life worth something.

Joy comes from long-term success in the areas that matter and will positively effect other people's lives for long-term good. So real joy cannot be achieved overnight. It is not fleeting, here one minute and gone the next. It is deeper. It comes from long-term habits that achieve long-term results.

> **You will be happy when your life helps others.**

These are not the things that happen overnight. It is years of investment in putting the interests of others ahead of your own. But when you live like this, you can't fail because you'll find that you have a crowd of people around you helping and holding you up. When you are down, those whom you have built up around you will help you. They will pick you up. You will try again. They will be behind you. You will succeed.

You have a foundation that cannot lose. You are a team. A team at home and a team at work. You stand with each other. You have learnt over time to trust others.

CHAPTER 9

Learn
to
Follow Up

*B*usiness is not about having an office. It is about having an assignment. When people start working for us and with us, the office is one of the last things we discuss. They join us because they want to do what we are doing.

> **I believe in transparency
> and availability.**

Offices should be places that are open and accessible to others, not a place that keeps you away from the people whom you are supposed to be working with and serving.

To really manage well, you need to be among the people you are managing. You need to know what is going on. Your job is not to be cut off from others. Managers need to come out of their office and follow up on their policies on the shop floor as it were, to see if they are the right policies and to see if they are working.

Poor managers rule by decree, but do not come out of their offices to follow up on what they have said. Poor managers govern by committees. The committee makes minutes and the job is considered done.

> **Our job is not to
> make minutes,
> but to
> get results
> and to make it work.**

The final responsibility is with the management, not with those we are responsible for. This is true not just for our work place or our business, but also for our home and family. The same principles apply. Are we accessible to our children? Do we listen? Are our policies the right ones? Do we know what is really going on in our children's daily lives? Are we following up on our instructions or are they just ceremonial? Do we mean what we say? Are we after real results?

Follow up. Find out if you are effective. Find out if your policies are working. Get away from your desk and relate to the people around you. Be interested in the lives of those you work with. Make sure you really know what your children are doing, who their friends are and what their problems are. Don't take such matters for granted, they are too important.

> **Don't be afraid of failure.
> You learn alot through failure.**

In one of the buildings we were erecting, we finished constructing the roof on the top floor. A person I knew sought the contract for felting the edges of the roof, where it joined to the gables.

He pleaded with me but I refused to give him the job. He asked whether I was his friend and I answered, *'Yes I am.'* But I said, *'You haven't failed enough at this kind of work yet. I only want some-one who has failed'*. He was surprised at my answer.

There are many wrong ways of doing a job like that. The way the rain comes down in the tropics you soon learn if it is done right or not, as you put buckets out to collect the water in your lounge room.

I told my friend, *'When you have failed on other people's buildings and you know what the potential pitfalls are, we will gladly employ you to work on our buildings'*.

I only employ people who have failed. These are the ones who are less likely to fail with us. In the long run, these will be cheaper to hire.

We employ people who come out of their offices, who know what is going on and where they have made errors in the past.

> **We all make errors.**
> **What we want**
> **are those people who learn**
> **from their errors.**

The principle of follow up is one of the most important I have seen in the lives of those who are effective. Some leaders operate as *'drive by administrators'*. As they drive by, everything looks like it is in order. If they came out of their car, looked around, opened their eyes, and looked under the carpet, they would find the seeds of a lower standard. They would find the termites and address the issue before the foundation is attacked.

One of our best staff in our West African operation, was not a big looking man. He was from
Uganda and had an East African accent. He
replaced another more important man who had
impressive formal qualifications. However, the
former man was unable to do the job as effectively
as the Ugandan. The Ugandan was always on the
job. He listened to the people, set his policy and
mixed among the people to find out what was going
on. He served over 1,600 people every day and
advised them, prayed with them, helped them and
governed them.

When people came to see him, they would ask
him to introduce them to his supervisor. They did
not realise that he was the one who led the depart-
ment. He did not look that impressive to them.
However, we discovered that '*being important*' can
sometimes cause you to miss out on what is going
on around you.

> ### What really matters is,
> ### are you doing what it takes to get
> ### the job done?

You may be in the office, you may have signed
the attendance book, you may have held all the
meetings and discussed all the problems and
strategies, but are you doing the job – the real job?

When I was younger, my boss often came to see
how things were going and would point things out to
me that were not right. Those things were not
included in my job description, but my boss knew
that if he showed me, they would get done. There
were others there that had more skill, but they
lacked the willingness to learn.

When a task is at hand there is no time for
excuses. What is needed is a solution. In Africa

you become solution conscious. Every day you will meet at least thirty main problems. If you have forty solutions, you will win. If you don't, you lose.

> ## If you can solve problems, you have the market.

The market will not listen to your excuses. You have to solve problems at a faster rate than they occur. You have to anticipate problems and cut them off before they occur. That is management. A manager has no right to be surprised. He or she should have been expecting the event.

By making effective follow up a part of your daily work habit, you will avoid many problems well in advance. This will help you to pave a better road to continual success.

CHAPTER 10

The Need for Discipline

*I*t is not easy to win a gold medal at the Olympic games. Certainly, no one can do it casually. To achieve at that level you have to develop your full potential.

This is because at that level the competition is very intense. Unless you have complete focus on what you are doing, you are not going to function at your best. 90% of your ability will not do. It must be 100% and more.

At that level you must regulate your lifestyle. Your sleep, your daily activities, your diet, your weight, your hobbies and exercise must all be regulated according to your coach's directives. This requires self-discipline.

What enables someone to have such discipline? Vision. The athlete's desire for that gold medal enables them to go to any extent necessary to compete in order to win. The desire to win enables them to summon the discipline that is necessary.

> ## Your vision of your goal disciplines every part of your being.

It is amazing what vision can do to bring discipline into your life. Vision can even affect your relationships. Developing a vision for a good marriage will start to govern the way you talk to your spouse. A vision for the future of your children will govern the way you treat them. Vision governs your life. You must have vision. Without vision you cannot have self-discipline.

Why is it so tough for the Olympian? Because at that level they are competing against the very best. In life we do not compete against other people, but we do compete against ourself. Each day we sharpen our vision. We make our goals clearer. This puts a harness around our life and brings out the very best.

Self-discipline starts with vision. It starts with dreams. You have to see yourself as an Olympian before you will ever come up with the determination to go through your training program. You must have hope.

> ## Hope gives you the strength to push through the tough times.

With your hope in place, you know that you have a purpose and that things will improve. You will not give up because you have a hope and a vision which you will not throw away.

Every great person has had a vision. It is the source of strength and discipline. But your vision should be a worthy one. It should include other people. Why do you want to be the best at something? Maybe you can be an example to young people, so that they can also achieve if they set their minds to it. You can show others that there is hope and that they do not need to waste their lives in mediocrity. You can be an example.

Discipline is a necessary factor in life. It is the cement that holds things together. It is an anchor that keeps you from straying off course. It is so good to have an anchor.

> **Discipline is the anchor that stops you from being lost.**

Being lost means that you are drifting around in the sea of life. The current takes you one way and then another. There is no purpose nor direction. No map, no blueprint. No signpost that shows you that you are on the right path.

A person without an anchor is moved from one decision to another by their feelings. They have no commitment. If they feel good today about something, they do it. If they feel good tomorrow about something else, they do that.

> **Success needs commitment.**

When you take up a project you must see it through to the finish. When you start something you must stay with it. This produces the character of a winner within you.

You may not always feel good about doing something, but in such times you have the commitment to take you through until your feelings change. You have an anchor that stops you from casting adrift in the currents of life.

Relationships are like this. You go through the tough times with people, because you are committed to relationships. You don't give up on someone because you are offended or you offend him or her.

Not only do you succeed when you have discipline in your life, but discipline is something you need to instill into the lives of those around you.

You do people a great favour when you teach them to be disciplined.

You must first become disciplined in your thinking. Other types of discipline will follow if your thinking is disciplined first. This is why it is so important to read and listen to the right material that will positively impact your life.

Don't let people talk about their rights all the time. Tell them about their responsibilities. To win you must take responsibility for each day.

> **Success will not come unless you learn to take responsibility for it.**

Train your children to be self-disciplined. Give them vision and hope for the future. Children are not easily fooled. If you are going to give them hope, it has to have a real foundation. You must be an example to them. They must first see it working in your life.

That is tough isn't it? Your children's future depends on you. Not what you tell them, but what you show them. It is worth it though. If you train your children to be disciplined, they will conquer their future.

Someone said, *'No pain, no gain'*. Vision gets

you through the pain. Always have vision. Don't ever let it be taken from you. Everything else can be taken, but never let anything take your vision. Vision keeps you alive. Vision needs to be passed onto the next generation.

A horse is no good without discipline. It may have power. But if it is just running around in the paddock, what good can come from it. You might like horses, but that doesn't mean that they should not fulfil a practical purpose. The harness disciplines the horse and channels the power of the horse towards a purpose.

You have one life. What are you doing with it? You have twenty-four hours a day. Does each day have a harness on it? Is the day directed towards a purpose?

Dynamite is no good when it blows up in mid air. It has purposeful power when it is packed under something. It must have a target and a specific purpose. Your life can be powerful if your activities are targeted towards a specific purpose. Each day that you work towards achieving that goal, you have power.

You need vision, dreams and commitment to use that power. Don't waste it here one day and there the next. Discover your purpose and get to work. Be disciplined.

CHAPTER 11

∞

Take Risks

J heard a man say that, *'Old people write wills and young people take risks'*. He said that the young say, *'If I perish, I perish'*. It is true that the young have little to lose. They have time to learn, time to experiment and they don't know that *'it can't be done'*. Age however must not stand in the way of your success, because age is a state of mind.

> **Risk is an essential ingredient to growth.**

You can never know for sure how something is going to work out. Calculate the *'likelihood's'* and then position yourself to take advantage of what you believe will be the future.

I remember a man who had far greater skills than I. He was handsome. He could sing beautifully. He could speak powerfully. He was educated. Nothing was stopping him except one thing. He would not take a risk. He always passed that buck to someone else.

> **Tomorrow's achiever
> will always be the one who picked
> up someone else's
> 'passed buck of risk' today.**

I remember making an investment in something that would take all my finances. My friend was amazed. He asked, *'How can you risk that? It is the last money that you have.'* I was equally amazed at his lack of foresight in seizing the moment.

I cannot understand it when people are too afraid to take risks. Risk is essential. The more risk you take the greater the rewards. Some people may think you have too much reward. They wouldn't think that way if they took the risks that you took.

I am not talking about foolish risk. I do not mean carelessness. Carelessness is irresponsible. Risk is not driving too fast. That is foolish. There is no benefit in that. That is not necessary risk.

Some say, *'You can't jump ahead; you have to take it one step at a time'*. I don't agree. If there is a river in front of you, you can't take that one step at a time. You may have to jump across to the other side.

> **There are times when not to
> take a risk is more risky
> than taking one.**

Once we had a period of six weeks in which to erect a new class and a new hostel. After six weeks, students would be back and the work had to be finished. One problem though, we only had enough money to start.

I told someone, *'I only have enough money to get myself into trouble'*. But we took the risk. Some of the money we needed came in. Then half way through the job it ran out. I remember looking at all the builders quietly thinking to myself, *'How am I going to pay them?'* None of them knew that I was thinking that.

But it worked. We made it to the other side. The two buildings were finished in six weeks and were fully paid for in cash. Within another two weeks, the new structures were full of students from 25 nations of Africa.

There was another time we were forced to take a risk. Nigeria was facing the prospect of civil war. Institutions were closing down around us. There was much trouble all around. Border wars were being fought between neighbouring nations while our students were away on a break.

The question was, should we close down or stay open? If war erupted, we could lose lives. If war did not erupt it would be hard to reopen. To communicate with thousands of people in different parts of Africa would be very difficult.

We stayed open. In the most difficult time I have ever experienced in my stay in Africa, we had the fastest and largest enrolment of students ever. People knew that we were stable. We won the market by taking a risk.

I am not suggesting that you go around doing stupid things. You had better study first. You better pray.

To grow you must take risks. Can you afford another child? Can you afford a good school for your children? You cannot perfectly predict the future. But that should not stop you working hard to provide the best.

A factor of parenthood is that you bear the

responsibility in taking risks that will benefit others. A father (or mother or a mature person) is one who has the practice of discerning when a risk is to be taken. The benefits are for others, but the responsibility is with the parent.

> **A leader takes risks.**
> **A leader bears the responsibility.**

When a leader fails, it may be classified as their fault. When they succeed, it is because the team succeeded. That is a good leader.

A leader has three qualities ...

⇨ Firstly, he or she knows where the group should be going.

⇨ Secondly, they know how to bring a group of people together to work towards that destination; they are good communicators.

⇨ Thirdly, they can properly organise the resources needed to get the job done.

> **In summary:**
> **Leaders have the correct vision.**
> **Leaders understand**
> **the needs of the**
> **people they work with.**
> **Leaders are good managers.**

Whether you are leading in a family, in the community or in a business, these are the qualities for successful leadership.

In all these three areas you are taking risks. Do you have the right vision? Does it coincide with your own skills? Will the people on your team work with you? Can you get the resources that will be needed?

You are a leader. You have a realm of responsibility. Everyone has responsibility to lead in some way and at some time. Leaders bear risk. Some abdicate that responsibility because they are adverse to risk.

Don't stick your head in the sand. If your community or your family needs leadership, stand up and give it. Yes, it is true that people stone leaders who fail. But you will stone yourself on the inside for never trying.

> **If you fail to try because of the fear of risk, you have already failed.**

The person who has failed is not the person who falls, but the person who will not try. They are the only failures in life.

> **No one who tries is a failure.**

Are you running away from something for fear of failure? If you are running, you have failed already by default. Face your fears and win.

CHAPTER 12

Role
Models

*B*efore you can lead a team you need to be a team member. This is where you gain experience. You learn what it's like working under the leadership of another. This is good preparation for your own future leadership roles. When you are a good follower you will know how to lead others better in the future. Others will then be more likely to follow you because you know what they are facing.

There are things that you are not able to learn in books. You need to learn them from other people.

> **Another person
> is a living example.**

By interacting with and learning from those who have gone ahead of you, you are able to see a living example.

Teachers know that people learn by what they read, by what they see and by what they do. In fact, the retention rate greatly increases when a student does. You retain far more by doing than by reading. Therefore, by watching someone else do what you want to do in life, and by doing it with them as a colleague and a friend, you learn so much faster. What you learn through this method of learning will stick with you.

What I am talking about here is training. It is one thing to study a book; it is another thing to be trained by a real person. When you are trained, the person stands by your side and watches you. When you are not *'putting the nail in the right place'* they tell you. A book won't tell you that. A book won't tell you if you are reading it correctly or not, but a person will.

You have to be willing to have this type of relationship with someone. If you don't like being told, then you are not going to be able to learn too easily from others. If it is going to offend you, you will have to go it alone. You will have to reinvent the wheel by yourself.

> **Choose a relationship**
> **that will assist you**
> **in the training process.**

Look at their life. Is that the type of life you want to have when you are that person's age? Don't just look at their financial situation, or their house or their car. Look deeper than that. Look at their character. Is that the type of character you want to have?

Look at the way the person treats other people. Is that the way you think other people should be treated? Look at the relationship they have with their spouse. Is it strong, happy and healthy? What about their children? How are they growing up? Don't just look at their house-help and say, *'I would like that too'*.

> ## Seek to understand
> ## your trainer's
> ## foundation.

When you go for the material things that the person has and you don't understand the person's commitment, their values and the underlying foundational principles, you are going to mess up. Look at the price the person paid.

These are pretty tough questions, but they are important. Unfortunately, we do not live in a perfect world. You will never find someone who will always meet your criteria of a perfect role model. However, these are still important questions.

As a parent, it is important to discover who your children use as role models. If their models are famous people, what type of lives do these people live? What type of values do these models portray to your children? You need to provide your children with the right type of role models. You need to talk to them about these things, so they can make judgements about who they follow.

You can learn alot from the people who have gone before you. You can start where they have finished and then build on top of that.

Look at the wars our parents went through. Look at the economic difficulties they went through, as the foundations for our current economies were set. They learnt hard lessons. Older people often struggle to share those lessons with following generations.

After World War II, people had respect for right values as they rebuilt their shattered lives. The wars were like a cleansing.

> ## Learn good values and keep them.

You are building a future for your family and those who follow you will learn from those who went before them.

Mechanics need to be apprenticed. They cannot learn only from books. They must have a car to work on, with an experienced mechanic by their side who can watch them and guide them.

If you have this type of relationship in your life, you are very fortunate. You should value it. If somebody is willing to spend this type of time with you, you should appreciate him or her for it.

> ## One of the best ways to help those who are helping you, is to achieve.

Remember they are not perfect, but you can find the good principles in their lives and follow them. You should not only do as well as them, but even better. You are starting from where they left off.

A role model is not somebody who makes decisions for you. They only show you principles. They train you by giving you encouragement and correction when needed. But only you make the decisions in your life.

> ## Making decisions remains your responsibility.

So find someone to stand by, to work with and help. While you are helping them, they will be giving you invaluable training; training you could never pay for. You will learn lessons that will be a great source of profit to you as you go through life. It is a living university of great value to you.

> **Only good followers make good leaders.**

Other people will follow you when you know how to lead. As you follow others, you will learn how to lead. You know how to build when you value the foundation that is laid by those who went before you. Build on their foundation and your building will stand strong.

CHAPTER 13

Have Foresight

*M*urphy's law states, *'If it can go wrong it will go wrong'*. I am not saying you should be negative. However, the person who plans to succeed covers himself against contingencies.

An achiever is a contingency thinker.

There is a Proverb that states, *'The prudent man foresees the evil and hides himself; but the simple pass on and are punished.'*

To *'hide yourself'* means that you do something about it. You anticipate what will happen before it happens and you take measures to cover yourself or to circumvent it.

So you need to have foresight. This is the ability to look ahead and anticipate different scenarios.

The simple person goes on his or her merry way and when something goes wrong they say they were not expecting it. They use this as an excuse for failing. Well they should have been expecting it. Why weren't they expecting it? Haven't they experienced life before? Some people refuse to learn from their past experiences.

My father used to tell me to do things in such a way that they are fail-safe.

> **Fail safe
> means that if it fails
> you are safe.**

If you are walking a tight rope and you have a net under you, you are safe if you fail. It is not prudent to walk on a tight rope without a net.

It is not negative to have a net under you – it is safe. You will only succeed if you survive long enough to do so.

The person who is prepared wins. He or she has anticipated what might go wrong and is ready for the event. They can then quickly fix the matter and get back on the track almost immediately.

You may have heard the expression, *'The one who fails to plan, plans to fail'*. Planning involves the consideration of likely events and how you can be properly prepared to meet and deal with them. If you aren't prepared to deal with events, they will deal with you.

In our educational institute in Africa we have to keep things moving all the time, fifty-two weeks a year. Because of the fragile state of the economy, it is always likely that we will not have electricity supply or water supply. It is probable that the telephone lines will not be operating. We have to organise fifty staff and lecturers and make sure that they are in the right place at the right time. We have to add to this their family members, to ensure all is well.

Then there are 10,000 meals to prepare every week. Then there is a large quantity of electronic equipment for sound in various lecture halls, lighting, computers and large trucks to move people and equipment. The present infrastructure of the nation means that anything can go wrong and break down at any time. All these things need to be working. If one area breaks down it slows up the whole work.

What attracts people to our work is that it is working – all the time. When some of our staff say that something should have been working but something else that they weren't expecting went wrong, I ask them, *'Why were you not expecting it?'*

It is a tough question, but it gets them thinking. I don't allow, *'I was not expecting it'* as an excuse. Many institutes allow excuses. Such institutes cannot rise to the top. I'm a firm believer that, *'You should have been expecting it.'*

You see, when you want to reach a goal, you must start by identifying your desired destination and then work back to plot how you are going to get there.

> **The first step to achieving a goal is to have foresight to know where you want to arrive.**

People who arrive late for an appointment often don't plan properly. If you have to arrive somewhere at 5:00 p.m. then the first question is, *'How long will it take for me to get there?'* Not the minimum time, but the probable time allowing for traffic and missing the road, if it is your first time to go there.

If you estimate the time you will have to leave, then you can determine the time you will have to start to get ready. Then you know how long you have to finish your current tasks before you start to get ready to leave for your appointment. You must start at the end goal and work back to plan how you are going to get there.

When you work on one of those pencil maze puzzles, they ask you to trace the way from the start to the finish. It is much quicker to start at the finish and trace your way back to the start. Start from where it is that you want to finish. Focus on the goal and the destination first.

When you want to catch a train to a certain destination, you start by firstly finding that destination on a map. Then you locate the train line it is on. You then find the stations you will have to change trains, in order to get on the correct line.

> **Start at the end and
> trace your way
> back to the start.**

The same process is applicable to how you should plan your life. Ask yourself the question, *'Where do I want to go?'* That is the only way you can determine what activities you should be working on today. You must have foresight.

Think about the effect of your actions before you take them. This is an important part of having foresight. Remember the goals you have in mind. They are not just about succeeding in business, but also in character, relationships and the impact your life will have on those people who are around you.

So before you act, remember that you are not just considering the immediate profit that may result. You are also determining the long-term impact the decision may have on others. You may make a profit, but is it ethical? If it is not, then how can you justify it before your children?

Some things are legal, but may not be ethical. How can you hope that your children will learn the right lessons in life and develop the right character unless they are firstly seeing it in you? You are their number one teacher.

So foresight is indispensable, especially when considering the long-term effects your actions will have. Not many have this type of foresight. Many have a sense of financial responsibility, but lack direction in developing the moral strength of character in their children.

You are not here just to provide your children with financial security. You are to provide them with a framework for living. You are to provide for them a guideline for moral and ethical decisions that they will make and which will determine their futures. You are the model.

CHAPTER 14

Work Your Way Out of a Job

$\mathcal{W}$hat I mean by working your way out of a job, is training others. Your attitude to having a position should not be *'how long can I keep this position for'*, but rather *'who can I train to know the things and the skills that I have?'* This attitude builds other people and it gives you more purpose to your life.

> ### Your goal in all your work should be to help others.

Again, this lifestyle requires a level of personal security. If your security or sense of self worth is in your position, then you will do everything possible to hold onto it. If your sense of value is in your job or title, you will be devastated if you lose your office.

When some people lose a job, it is not just their

income they lose. They lose their sense of value. Unless they are the breadwinners they feel worthless. It is true that we all desire to be needed by others and to be useful to other people, but our sense of security must rest on something more stable than our exploits for any given day.

> **No position you hold can ever change who you are as a person.**

When people recognise your efforts, it's nice. But it shouldn't determine the opinion you have of yourself.

Many people lack a real sense of security and it often causes them to become controllers. Living only to maintain what you have will not release you to achieve at your maximum level. It will also hinder your ability to properly train others and to help them to achieve at their maximum level. Your vision will be too narrow and too limited.

> **You must see beyond what you are doing now, to what you could be doing in the future.**

With a clear vision of your future in your mind, you will have a more liberal attitude towards mentoring other people.

So much of life is about training others. When you hold any position, one of your goals should be to train at least one other person to do your job. You should be passing on all the knowledge you have to other people. When their turn comes, they can start from where you finished and improve on it. Don't worry that they will do a better job. Don't worry whether they will give you the credit for their success. You will have the inner satisfaction that you have done the right thing.

Some try to keep their skills as their own secret. This is to ensure that they remain needed. This is poverty mentality. Such people think that if they lose their job they won't get another one. They do not believe that their skills and work ethic will open up new doors and brighter prospects. In short, they do not live positive believing lives. When they finally pass on, they will not be remembered for '*being a blessing to many*'. Such people will never reach their full potential.

> ## Your full potential is only reached as you train others.

As you impart what you know and who you are into someone else, you are realising your full potential through that person.

On your own, you'll live one life and die. That's it! However, if you train others your life will continue to live on through them. What they achieve throughout their life, you will have achieved through them. This is the way to ultimate achievement. You may not get the immediate credit for it, but you will know that you did it. The person you trained will train the next generation and on it will go. For many years into the future your life will be making a difference. You will be positively affecting lives for many years after you are dead and gone.

You might think that this is a bit too far-fetched, thinking of generations ahead. Of course this philosophy may not pay your bills at the end of this week, but it will give you a lot more satisfaction in life.

> ## To live life to the fullest, you need to think ahead.

Alot of the time people only think of the imme-diate, the emergency and the short term. Many live perpetually with their focus on the needs of this week only. They don't invest in the future.

So how do you make a positive change? Take another person and teach him or her. Pass on to them what you know. Train them to do the job that you are doing. Care about their life. Look for someone who has the character and the desire to go ahead and invest time into that person's life. It may not be a lot of time. Maybe a bit of time here and a bit there. But every bit will make all the difference. Look for an opportunity to give someone a lesson here and an explanation there.

One of my greatest motivations is to see the *'light turn on'* in someone else's head. I love to see people understand things that they did not know before. It gives me great satisfaction. I am especially happy when I have trained someone up who I now believe can do my job. It means I am ready to move onto something else. It means that I am not condemned to the same office and job year after year. It means I can now go on to other things.

Don't ever allow your work to be a stagnant thing. You should have a positive outlook towards it. It is not a job you land or a business you own in which you must settle down for a predictable future. It is not your *'security'*. You should see your work as an ever evolving and ever changing learning experience.

Work forms at least one third of your entire life. Why spend a whole lifetime on earth and have no vision or satisfaction? Life is more than a pay packet. Allow your work life to become an ongoing discovery.

**Work is a large part of your life,
so live it to the fullest.**

Take the risk. Train someone else to do your

job. Don't stagnate. Don't allow those around you to stagnate. Get a hold of the person next to you and teach them something. Reach out to them and give them good advice. If you have discovered something that is good and works for you, then give it to someone else.

Do this for your children first of all. There is no point having many people thanking you for teaching them when your own children can't remember the last time you sat down and read them a book or showed them a skill.

> **Your children are the most important ones that you should mentor.**

The purpose of life is to train others. One day you won't only leave your office but you will also leave this life. Who will take over when you leave? Are you training them now? Will they be entertainment minded, mere consumers and pleasure seekers, or will they have real values that will guide them safely through the minefield ahead?

> **Training others is your responsibility.**

CHAPTER 15

Learn to Persevere

*Y*ou need to develop an attitude of gratitude. When you are grateful for life it helps to release the right thought processes for creative thinking and ideas.

Be grateful for where you are today. Be grateful for the life that you have. There are people who are in a much worse situation than you are at present. No matter what has gone against you, learn to be grateful for life.

When you eat a peach be grateful for it. Think about that peach. There are alot of things you want to achieve in life, but could you make a peach? Look at how well made it is, how nice it tastes, and how juicy it is. The seed of life is in it. After enjoying the peach you could take the seed and start a peach business. Think about that peach. It is a gift to mankind. You didn't make it, but there it is, a free gift to you. Be grateful.

Don't work because you are driven to it by jealousy of other people's success. Don't work hard in fear that you might not succeed. These things do not release good ideas that are beneficial to others.

Don't think you deserve an easy ride or that it must have been easier for others. Don't get into self-pity or become a whinger. Whingeing kills success. The law of gravity applies to all people. Life is not picking on you.

Never give up. That is the only rule in wanting to succeed. Have a goal and a plan and then embark on it. Once you have embarked, never give up. Learn from your mistakes, adjust yourself and go again. Never give up.

> **Persevering means
> that you
> will never give up.**

You will try again. It is only when you stop trying that you fail. No one who is trying is a failure. A failure is the person who feels sorry for him or herself or who makes excuses.

Denial is one of the worst enemies of change. When you deny that you have a problem then you will not try to discover the solution to it. Some people never change year after year because they will not recognise that there is a fault.

> **Denial is something that
> you have to be
> on guard against.**

I knew a man who wrote a book called, *'I Choose to Change'*. He didn't just choose once, but it was a continuous choice to change. When you have finished changing then you have finished growing. Don't get stuck in a rut. When you need to change you need to admit it.

In our College in Africa, we lecture in three different languages; English, French and Hausa. The countries around us are mainly English and French speaking. The people of the sub-Sahara region speak Hausa.

We persevere at this work year after year so that our impact as a College will not be limited to one nation. Only through consistent perseverance can we educate people who will have a positive impact on their nations, no matter where they come from on the whole continent of Africa. We are determined that our graduates will impact lives in every single nation throughout the continent.

It is not an easy thing to support staff and their families, so that lectures can be provided for all our courses in three separate languages. It is costly to have the building space to separate the College into three different language groups. It takes alot of careful work to translate all our course texts into two different languages and to print thousands of copies every year, year after year. It takes perseverance.

You can have an impact through achieving goals. You can have multiplied impact by persevering in your success year after year. Perseverance causes your success to multiply. It keeps on impacting more and more people as you get better and better at what you are doing.

**When you are good at something,
keep going at it until you are better.
When you are better,
keep working at it until you are
the best that you can be.**

Then keep doing it. You can have a positive

impact on so many people. Don't stop now.

If you believe that your goal is valid and that it is worth fighting for, because it is helping others, then you will do it. You will achieve it.

When you persevere, you will break through and bring it to pass. You will not grow tired from the obstacles. Obstacles will become the stepping-stones to your success, rather than reasons to stop.

> ### Those who are sure of what they want will win in life.

You may think you want something, but if the price is too high to get it you may change your mind. Do you really want your life to make a difference to others? Do you really want your life to be a help to others? Then you have to persevere. That must be your decision.

It is when you come to obstacles and to knock backs that you will really begin to discover whether what you want and what you think is really important to your life. Do you want to get ahead or do you just want to live an ordinary life?

You have the chance in this life of growing and being a help to many others. Is that what you want or will you allow the obstacles of life to eat away at your dreams? Will you persevere? Do you really know what is important in life? Are you willing to fight for it, or have you already retired on the inside of yourself?

> ### Perseverance is the key to realising your goals.

Many people have good dreams. Many people have skills and many people have opportunities, but none of these things are enough. Successful people persevere until they get what they are after. It doesn't matter how many times they are set back, they keep coming back. You cannot stop them. They keep coming back. Eventually they get the break that they need because they never give up.

You will get what you desire. But to do so you must lock in on it. You must strip yourself of all excess weight and distractions to enable you to focus on the one thing. Then you must persevere at that one thing until you achieve it. You will achieve it.

CHAPTER 16

Be Determined

$\mathcal{G}$etting a good idea is one thing, but bringing the idea into reality is another. It is a bit like being pregnant. Between the time of conception and delivery, there is a lot of work. There is time and there is effort. However, it is good effort because you love the baby.

> **Love makes the effort worthwhile.**

Good ideas are like the baby. You love them. You nourish, develop, think on and perfect them. The idea is your baby. But it takes a lot of effort to bring it into reality. But you don't mind the effort, because it is your baby. You know it is going to come to pass.

Once you have an idea there is a right time for implementing it. To succeed, it must be implemented at the right time and in the context of the right surrounding circumstances.

Every great man and woman has had to have the right circumstances or opportunity in history for his or her greatness to appear. Without the failure of the French revolution, Napoleon might have never been known. Without the Second World War, Winston Churchill may have never been Prime Minister of Britain. People didn't like him. He had too many rough edges. They called him a bulldog. But there came a time when Britain needed a bulldog.

> **Idea people
> have to be
> conscious
> of their
> environment.**

The timing, the opportunities, the right market and surrounding circumstances all affect the implementation of an idea. An idea never works by its own right. It must fit into its environment. You must be environment sensitive. What is the right idea for your place and time?

But just because the time is right, it doesn't mean that your idea is going to automatically come to pass. It probably won't at first. Not many great ideas have worked on the first attempt. It is usually only those who refuse to give up, who refuse to be put back and who work through every obstacle along the way, who get through.

> **Success is not necessarily automatic.
> It may require some manual labour.**

We live in an instant age. But ideas never materialise instantly. They always take a lot of refining to get it right. Just because your idea didn't work on the first fifty attempts, doesn't mean it is not a good idea.

So don't allow yourself to be discouraged. *'Dis-couraged'* means that your courage is taken. Negative thinking is what removes your courage. Think that you will make it and it will give you courage.

Courage comes from the way you think.

If something is worth doing then stick at it. Don't be a *'jack of all trades and master of none'*. Decide what goals in life are worthwhile and then go for it. Become a master in that area. Over time, you will become invaluable to others. You will become an expert in your field. If something is worth doing then it is worth sticking at.

Become a sticker. Don't allow anything to deter you. Have the reputation that others will say of you, *'Well you know her, if she starts something then she will finish it'*. If you start something, finish it. It is a good habit. Develop the habit of sticking with something until it is finished. Be a finisher.

When you have finished one task then you will experience the good feeling of having completed a job well done. You can then move onto the next task. When you develop that as a habit then you become an achiever.

**An achiever is simply someone
who finishes things.**

An achiever sticks at things. They are not an electrician one day and a bank clerk the next. Become an expert at something. Work at it until you know everything there is to know about it. Be better at your job than anyone else. Be the best at what you do. Know it inside and out.

Achievement will take care of itself when you develop the habit of finishing things. You don't have to be great to be an achiever. Just finish things and you will be an achiever.

> ## To achieve you only need to develop the right habits.

You need to be determined when other people don't understand you and what you are doing. Sometimes people will say that you will never make it. Sometimes you will be on your own. No one may be willing to agree with what you are doing. This will be a test of your determination.

Sometimes you will see something that no one else around you can see. They may be focused in on other things. They may not have the time to look at what you are looking at. There may be too many risks involved in what you are aiming at. People may not be sure that you will make it. They may not want to be responsible for encouraging you. There will be times when you want encouragement but you will just have to encourage yourself, because sometimes only you have the vision.

You have to make a judgement about the risk you are going to take. If you believe you are right then you have to encourage yourself and then be determined. Don't give up.

> ## Live long enough to prove your critics wrong.

Be determined. Be patient. Time changes many things. If you stick with it long enough and don't jump out, you will make something of your goals and of yourself.

Among the most determined people I have ever met are many Africans I know. Many of my friends there cannot be discouraged and they will not take no for an answer. No matter the odds against them they believe in yes – yes, it can be done. They believe there is a way and that they will find it. When you tell them that it can't be done, they say, *'My case is different'* and they believe it. They keep trying until they get it.

This is an admirable character quality. When someone cannot be discouraged, they have an admirable character quality. No matter what comes against them they won't get bitter or complain. Their eyes are fixed on their target and they won't give up until they reach it.

> **Stop complaining and start complying.**

Do what needs to be done to get through. Be determined. Get up and go again. Stop saying, *'It isn't fair'*. That is one thing I will not allow my children to say.

You can't go through life saying it isn't fair. One of life's rules is, *'Success is not handed to you on a silver platter'*. So don't complain about it. Let your attitude comply with it. Then you will be motivated. You will be physically and mentally alert and astute to make the fullest use of every day. Have an attitude to work. Don't think you are going to get a free ticket. There is no such thing.

CHAPTER 17

Maintenance

*M*aintenance is one of the inevitable words of life. Life must be obtained and then maintained. You cannot just be a dreamer and a frontier person breaking new ground.

> **You are going to have to maintain whatever ground you take.**

Throughout the centuries, many have tried to overtake Russia. Napoleon took ground by heading into the interior of Russia at lightning speed. He took huge areas of land, but he wasn't able to consolidate. When winter set in, he was not in a position to maintain. His army suffered a devastating loss. Russia's biggest defence was, *'You might be able to take us quickly, but you can't maintain it. We will just wait it out'*.

Hitler studied the battles of the past to try to learn how it could be done. But again he was forced into a premature advance upon Russia. He took large areas of land, but again he could not hold it when winter set in. His army also suffered huge losses.

You have heard the saying, '*Don't bite off more than you can chew*'.

It is one thing to make quick advances, but can you maintain the new responsibilities?

You can borrow a large sum of money to gain a speedy advance, but can you pay the monthly commitments?

Whether it is a loan or any other type of responsibility, advancements always bring with it an increase in monthly commitments. This is called maintenance.

Working in Nigeria is hot. At 3:00 a.m., you are lying on your bed with a fan turning over your head, but still you are in a pool of sweat. In our offices, we also used fans, but they were not sufficient to deal with the very high humidity levels. So after some time we were able to buy an air conditioner. We rejoiced. Then we were able to buy another and another and many more.

Our advancement did not stop there. We bought one computer and then another and another and more. Then generators and intercom systems, photocopiers, video camera equipment and then high quality sound equipment, vehicles and on and on.

You can rejoice in all these advancements, but it only means that your monthly commitments, obligations and stress level will increase with it. You find out that the more you advance the more you need to maintain it.

Victory can be a dangerous thing. Victory too

soon or ahead of time can lead to a set back. Not that you shouldn't expect and work for great victories, but are you ready for them? Have you counted the cost of the commitment? What are you going to do to maintain it? Have you thought about that – properly?

It is easy to get ahead, but can you stay there? Anyone can make quick advances, but can you hold the ground. An army needs a strong supply line to hold ground, or it will find that it has gone in too far and has over reached itself. You need to think like an army thinks – don't advance beyond the ability of your nation to keep you supplied. Unfortunately, Generals do not always have the luxury of a choice in this matter. Circumstances press them into taking chances.

> **Your effort in life is 20% advancement and 80% maintenance.**

If you are not a maintainer, or not maintenance minded, you are not going to hold territory.

> **Holding is more important than taking.**

There are many things that need maintenance. Relationships are the most important. But you don't maintain relationships for the sake of your work. That is insincerity and people can see it a mile off. You maintain relationships for the relationship's sake itself.

In our work in Africa, two main areas need to be maintained. One is the student inflow. This requires recruitment all over Africa. It also requires that the students, currently in the school, receive the best education possible. That is where we put our funds.

We do not advertise. We look after our students. They are our best advertisement. They go all over Africa and the world telling everybody about the College, and we don't pay for it.

We erected beautiful signboards with fountains and gardens, all showing the name of our College. Thousands of people take their photo in front of them and send the photos to thousands of different locations. We don't pay for that, but it advertises the College far more effectively than any advertising campaign could do in that type of continent. So we maintain our inflow of students by making the ones we have strong and healthy.

The second area we need to maintain is the income side. We have to pay for that. Most of it does not come from the students. Many of them need help. They need a start. They need a kick-start in life – someone who will believe in their potential when it is not yet revealed.

That money has to be raised. So the more you grow, the more it costs to maintain. When we raise a large amount of money to build a large building we then, after it is built, have to maintain it and finance the students to fill it and the staff to teach in it. It's costly, but it is worth it. Lives are being changed as they are being educated.

Maintenance is harder than the original advance. Many people get excited when there is a new big project on. People will contribute towards that. But when the project is finished, not as many people will get as excited about the daily, monthly, and annual maintenance of that vision.

What is the point of the big project unless it is maintained year after year? There is no point to it unless it does the work on a daily basis. That is where *'the rubber hits the road'*. This is where commitment is needed. This is the unseen, unexcitable and real work.

It is not so easy to get excited about maintenance. You may want the next big breakthrough but you have to keep everything running.

**A good manager keeps everything
in working order every day.**

This is what distinguishes a good company from a bad one. The one that can keep everything running day in, day out is the company that will take over the market.

80% of your work is good maintenance. Yes you need the right product and the right opportunities, but when you have an advantage in the market place, you must maintain your standard. This is where many big companies fall down. They get too big and too bored to maintain their standard of service. You find after a while that their smile is skin deep. Their standard of service has gone. It won't be long before another up and comer has taken the market.

**Anyone can build something,
but keeping it going is the key.**

CHAPTER 18

Dreaming

*S*omebody once asked me the question ...

> **'What would you plan to do if you knew
> that you could not fail?'**

If the possibility of failure were removed, then what plans would you make? How big would you think?

People are often afraid of failure, so they think in restricted terms. Failure governs their thinking and thus their creativity is always within certain bounds.

Children are not experienced enough to know what cannot be done. It is lovely telling a small child some far-fetched thing and they believe you. They believe you because you are their parent and they trust that you ought to know. I do not mean that you leave them believing something false. I am just highlighting a point.

> ## Children are trusting. Learn from them.

Adults lose this ability to believe. They have experienced failure and this governs their ability to dream. We need to be more like the child. We should be less cynical and more of a possibility thinker.

So what would you plan if you knew you could not fail? The only way you will know that is to dream a bit more. Yes you need to have your feet on the ground. You need to be practical minded. But that comes after you have dreamed. You also need to be a dreamer. So try it.

> ## Remove failure from the equation and begin to dream of what you would like to be, do and achieve.

Dream in line with what your talents are. You are not somebody else. You are you. You may not have the other person's skills. You may never be like them. Don't wish to be like someone else.

You have certain talents and skills that are unique to yourself. You can dream dreams that no one else can dream. But when you dream, dream in line with what your character is, what YOU would like to do and with what you are good at.

Don't be ashamed of yourself – dream. You have already achieved in the past.

> ## Dream how you can expand on your past achievements and then do more.

You have already used certain skills. Dream of a wider door of opportunity, to use the same skills in a bigger way.

There are two sides to your intellect. One is the analytical; to work out the details. The other helps you see the bigger picture. You need to function in both of these realms.

If someone said to you that they would supply the money and that money would be no problem, what would you do? What would you plan and what dreams would you formulate? Now that money is not the issue, what would you dream?

You say, *'Well now you're talking'*. No, I was talking before. You just didn't hear it. Money should not limit your dreams. It has nothing to do with what you are dreaming about. Forget about money. Concentrate on what you want to do.

What would be a very good and great thing for you to do? Think about it. Dream about it. Meditate on it until it gets bigger and clearer. Make this a habit. Your dreaming must get clearer and clearer and clearer, until you have a very clear picture.

Your picture must be clear. This doesn't usually happen all of a sudden but the more you dream the clearer it gets.

> ## When the dream becomes clear then it becomes possible.

Many people stop dreaming before it becomes clear. They see a problem or they think about the money and they stop dreaming. Don't think about the money. Wait until you have a long clear picture of what it is you want to do.

Money always goes towards the best idea. People who have money are looking for the best idea. That is the problem about having money – what to do with it? You ask anyone who has it.

So you don't need the money, you need the idea. Money will come once you have the idea.

Don't dream with self-imposed limitations. Dream first what you would like to do. If it is a good purpose and will benefit others then it is a good dream.

Once you have a good idea about your dream, now is the time to start dreaming about the financing of that dream.

> ### Take your
> ### dreaming one step at a time.

Know what you want to do before you dream about how to do it. Dream about how to do something before you sit down to work out how to do something.

When you have a dream about how to finance something then you can sit down and call the people and make the negotiations to work out the details. Dream clearly before you work it out.

> ### You must dream clearly.
> ### Then you must work it out
> ### precisely.

Dream about your objectives first. Dream about the financing later. The money will come if you already have a clear picture of what you will do with it and if you are ready.

Many people are not ready because they think that nothing good could ever happen to them. So they have given up real dreaming. If you were suddenly given a few million dollars, do you know what you would do with it? Have you been dreaming? Do you have a plan? If most people had that much money they would have no idea where to start.

If you gave me that much money I would know within half an hour what I was going to do with it. I already have a plan that is bigger than that. I am ready. It would take more than many millions for me to fulfil all I am dreaming about. So if you gave me a few million I would immediately know exactly how to use it. I would put it to use in helping others and I would have a lot of good fun doing it.

> **So dream big about helping others and get ready to do something big about it.
> One step at a time your dreams will come true.**

CHAPTER 19

Persistence

*I*f you don't ask you will never know. If you don't look you will never find. Some people are too afraid to ask questions and too timid to continue probing until they get the answers. They are put off by the mean manner of people who are tired and fed up at their 9 to 5 jobs.

> **Persistence means
> you continue.**

You will never do this if you are timid. Don't worry about looking '*out of place*' because you don't know something. If you don't admit it, put your hand up, and ask a question, you will never know.

Those who persist find a way when there is apparently no way. When one way closes they do not say, '*Well it cannot be done*'. They say, '*Another way will open up*'. They know that it can be done. Even if it looks like every way is closed, they know inside themselves that there is a way.

> **When one way closes another way will open.**

You just have to find it. You just have to believe that it is there. It doesn't matter how you feel about it.

Stop feeling depressed about it. Answers do not come in the midst of depression. Depression can kill a thousand good ideas a minute before they get a chance to conceive. A depressed person will refuse to allow an idea to germinate.

Stop. Start looking. Start searching. Start studying.

> **You will find answers to everything if you really want them.**

Some people don't really want answers because they are not willing to face them. They don't want to change their life. They say they want the answers, but they don't. When you give them the answers they argue with them and say they are still searching. They are not searching. They have already given up on life because they don't want to face up to the need to change.

Unbelief is easier for them – they think. But it is really the hard way, because they go on and on without putting the real answers to work in their life; in their marriage, family, business and relationships. Life for them is hard and bitter and they go on complaining about it.

> **Desire will get you out of the mire.**

Do you desire to find a way through the difficulties you are facing or not? Do you desire it enough? If you do, then you will not give up. When the events of life test you to see what you really want, you will answer with, *'Yes I want it!'* Is that how you answer? When life asks you that question you must answer with a big, *'YES, I am ready. Whatever it takes, don't count me out. I am in.'* If you don't answer like that then forget it.

Don't be timid about persisting. If someone doesn't give you the answer you need at first, then ask again. Don't have the *'Excuse me for living'* attitude. *'I will stop bothering you and go away and leave you alone now'*. No, don't leave people alone. If you need to make a call, then make it. Don't be put off by their official *'better than thou'* attitude.

No one is better than you. Learn to persist. Think right.

I remember a *'Once upon a time'* story my father told me to illustrate this.

There was a man driving in the country late at night. He had a flat tyre, but his car jack had been loaned out to another person. So he began to walk to a neighbour's farmhouse to ask for a loan of a jack.

On the way he began to think about how late it was. He thought his neighbour might be asleep, since he had to get up early the next morning to milk the cows. He thought his neighbour might be angry about being woken up so late.

As he continued to think about this, he thought that it was unreasonable that his neighbour should be angry about being woken, considering the circumstances. The more he thought about this the more judgmental he became of his neighbour.

By the time he reached his neighbour's house and knocked on the door he was convinced that his friend would give a negative reply. As his friend opened the door with glazy tired eyes, the man who had the flat tyre yelled at him for his lack of helpfulness and understanding, slammed the door and went back towards his car without the help that he needed. The neighbour had no idea what was going on.

Is that how you knock on doors? With some people, you only have to open the door an inch and they stick their foot in. Others already believe they will not be allowed in before the door is answered.

That is the way some people think about the doors that they need to knock on in life. They have a negative attitude about it before they even start. They are afraid of getting a *'no'* from the person. They think that a *'no'* would be the worst embarrassment that they could face.

So instead of risking a *'no'*, many people don't ever ask. They go on in life without knocking, without asking and without searching. They think that if they tried and it didn't work, they will have wasted their time.

> **You might get a thousand no's and then one YES.
> That is all you need.**

Well you have to persist, regardless of your feelings. You will probably find that your neighbour is delighted to help you – yes, you! You will find that you will get the answer that you need, but you must persist.

The Bible says, *'If you know how to give good gifts to your children, how much more will your Heavenly Father give good gifts to you'*. This gives me a great motivation for persistence.

If you have children, I trust you are good to them. You make sure they have breakfast and the things that they need. You desire for them to have a good future and provide it in the best way that you can. Well, do you think that life will treat you with any less kindness than you know is right for your own children?

So have some courage. Get up and persist. You will find a way through. The way through is there. Just don't give up before you reach it. Don't give up just before your break is about to happen.

Get out and knock on doors. If you are not knocking, then it is sure that none will open for you. You have already cancelled yourself out by default. Get out and knock. It will open. Life will work for you. The world is not against you. You are no different to anyone else who succeeded. They all had their faults – more than you. Thinking you are different is the only fault that cannot be helped.

> **You will win if you are in it.**
> **To be in it you must persist.**

CHAPTER 20

Delegation

*T*he best way to get ahead is to empower other people who are working with you. This is called delegation. When you delegate, you are granting another person the power to make decisions and to act on your behalf. In doing so, you are giving some of your power to others.

If you don't know how to give freely, you will never know how to do this either. Some people just can't give freely, unless there is something in it for them. However, when you can give you can grow. Giving allows you to extend far beyond your limitations.

Some people have a problem with delegation. Often they find it hard to trust people. Sometimes when they delegate they take back their authority at the crucial moment. The person they delegated to finds that they don't really have the power. They realise that they are just an incapacitated worker who does not really know what is going on.

There have been times when I have delegated

power even when I have not agreed with the decisions that the other person has made. Other staff have asked me to intervene and reverse the decisions of others. But at such times I have resisted and explained to staff that delegated power is delegated power. Once a staff member has made a decision then we go with it. In this way we allow respect and value to be given to each member of our team.

Now there are times when a staff member may make a definite error that will bring harm to the work. At such a time you should step in and make a correction. You should explain to the staff why you have to intervene and correct. They should understand very clearly why you are doing that. They should understand that you are consistent and in this case you are right to bring in a correction. You should never do it in such a way that humiliates them.

> **If you have delegated power
> to someone,
> that person should feel secure
> in his or her position.**

If they think that you are going to come in at anytime and take back that power, move the goal posts and humiliate them, then they will be scared to make decisions and scared to commit themselves on any issue. They will not really believe they have the power even though you have assured them that they do. They will not really believe you. What you say and what you are, are two different things.

> **If you get delegation right, you will increase
> your effectiveness in a multiplied manner.**

Some people add to their successes. It is better to multiply your successes and I know that most people would rather multiply than add. You multiply by training and releasing others.

Delegation is not only needful in business, but also in the family and in almost everything that you do. How are your children going to grow up and mature unless you delegate to them? How will they ever learn how to make decisions unless you give them the opportunity to learn?

Sometimes when you delegate it is *'costly'*. For people to learn, you have to allow them a certain area where they can make mistakes. You make sure the mistakes are not too big and damaging, but you must allow them that opportunity.

> **You must give people a chance to learn.**

People cannot grow without experience. Guide them through it. But you don't just throw someone out there on their own and say, *'Well it's up to you now'* and walk off and leave them. No, you have to train them. You have to sit down and teach them and work with them until they understand what it takes and what they will have to do.

It is a dangerous world. You don't just throw your children out there and say, *'It's time for you to grow up buster'*. No, they have to be prepared. When you delegate, you have to prepare the person and train them for the job.

When you delegate, you allow the other person to get used to making the decisions. You give them feedback on how they are doing. Show them what they are doing right and how they can improve in various areas in which they have been acting. Don't publicly disgrace them. Publicly assert them.

> **Anyone to whom you delegate must trust you.**

Trust is the most important factor in any relationship, especially between you and the people who work with you. You cannot always determine the parameters of the relationship with those you work under, but you can learn from them and determine how you will build your relationship with those to whom you delegate.

Consistency is the key to effective delegation.

At home, your children must know where you stand, what you think about certain matters and what you would do in certain situations. When your children trust you, that you don't react in an unpredictable manner, then they will feel secure. They will grow up and mature in an environment like that. So will those who work with you. It is governed by the same principles.

When you delegate to someone, you don't dictate the decisions that they will make. You say, '*I would do it this way*' or '*When I was in your position, this is how I did it*'. But you then tell them that it is their work now and ask them how they think it should be done. Discuss their answer with them. Ask them why and point out any reservations or any matter they may have overlooked.

You don't tell the person what decisions to make, but you tell them the philosophy of what the team is about. They should know your vision. It should not just be your vision. It should be the vision of the whole team. Ask them what their vision is for the work. Discuss it with them and come up with a vision that everybody on the team has contributed towards.

> **A good leader brings out the best in the people on their team.**

So you don't tell the person what to do. You share with them the vision and the philosophy of the team. When they know the direction and the vision of the whole then they will make the right decisions to move everything forward in the right direction.

When you deal with people in this way, you bring the best out of them. When they are secure and they know that it is their work and that you are there to support them, they will take chances. They will stick their neck out and look for innovative ways to move their team forward. These are the type of people you want to be working and living with in your business and in your family.

Your children need to be living like this. Let them be secure. Encourage their good points. Teach them principles and help them to make their own decisions as they start to get older. When they are wrong correct them. But most importantly, teach them the principles of life.

CHAPTER 21

Giving

J was once told, *'When you climb the ladder, leave the ladder there for someone else to climb after you'*. This is the right attitude to have concerning advancing yourself. If you are so scared about competition that you knock down the ladder in order to stop others from climbing up after you, then you have cut off the help that you will later need yourself. Giving gives you a liberal spirit.

> **When you give, it is yourself that you are helping more than anyone else.**

This means that giving is a privilege. Don't give as though you were the master and the person you're giving to is the lesser. No, giving is a privilege. It helps you when you give. Be thankful for the opportunity you have to give into someone else's life and projects.

Giving produces a liberal spirit. It frees you up on the inside. That releases the *'juices'* inside you that promote free thinking and creativity.

> ## He who gives freely – thinks freely.

When you give to others then you do not feel bad about receiving from others. None of us can make it on our own. We all need help. So when you learn to give then you also learn to receive. You are not a self-made man or woman. You are part of a community of people who share and promote the interests of each other. You live in the *'win-win'* mode of thinking and acting.

When you learn to give freely, you are not just giving to those from whom you hope to receive some favour in return. Giving is not something you use to get yourself *'well connected'*. You give to people whom you can help, regardless of whether they are able to help you in some other way at some other time. This is true liberality.

The biggest joy in life is not what you have achieved and it is not what possessions you have amassed. These things do not measure the quality of your life nor of your value as a person.

> ## It is what you give that measures your life.

You need to have more than what you yourself need, so that you can help others get up on to their own feet and have a go at life. That is what makes life worth living.

> ## Giving becomes easy when you realise what has been given to you.

Some boast in their own qualities and forget that they have nothing that was not given to them.

If you are handsome or beautiful, did you make your hair or facial features? Did you form your nose and colour your eyes? Did you make yourself the height that you are or form the muscle tissue that allows you to run fast?

Every Wimbledon tennis champion was able to win because they had faculties that they were born with and did not make for themselves. Their very life was a gift. Yes they trained. They worked hard and disciplined themselves. They set goals and were determined to achieve them. But life itself for them was a gift.

Even the commonsense you use to pick yourself up by your bootstraps and win in life is a gift. You say you were determined and that you worked hard. Yes you did, but the brain you have which gave you the intelligence to do these things and make these decisions was not made by you. Did you make your brain or was it given to you?

> **Life is a gift.**
> **So too are your victories in life.**

We have the privilege of being able to work hard. We also have the privilege to overcome the obstacles and to train ourselves at life and win. The titles you have won are a gift. Yes you have worked for them, but life on earth was given to you, including the opportunity to do these things.

If what you have was given to you, then you ought to be able to give to others. If you cannot boast in what you have achieved, then you will have a free heart to help others achieve.

> **When boasting is gone,**
> **a helping hand**
> **begins its work.**

Ask anyone who has become so rich that they don't know what to do with their money. Life becomes meaningless for them. They turn to giving. Life for them is how they can help others to get meaning in their life.

> **When you help others to achieve meaning in their life, then you will achieve meaning in your own life.**

When you know that you have been given a second chance, then you will allow people around you to have a second chance. When you realise that people have been kind to you, then you will have no option but to be kind to others. When you realise that you have been forgiven of many things, then you will be forced to forgive others, even of many things.

> **Giving people a second chance – that is part of giving.**

Give people a chance to explain themselves. Give them another chance to get up and make something of their lives – even when they have wasted chances before.

Give people a clean slate, *'You owe me nothing, I forgive you'*. Saying that to others, even when it is hard for you, will free you up. It is not those you hold a grudge against that hurt, it is you. It is you that lies awake at night full of acid in your stomach, not the other person. When you decide to forgive, it is yourself you help. You are the one that is set free.

To forgive is a choice. There is no such thing as *'I can't'*. It is your choice. After you have made that choice then you can choose how you will think about it.

> **You are what you think.**

You can choose how you will think. That choice will determine what you become in life.

CHAPTER 22

Team Work

$\mathcal{T}$eamwork requires an interdependent attitude and lifestyle. In contrast, the independent person relies on his or her own strengths alone. This type of person doesn't like to ask others for help. They go it alone.

Interdependence means that we join together as a team and we share our strengths with each other. Where you are strong, you help me. Where I am strong, I help you. The way of getting ahead is to identify the areas where you need help. Instead of hiding them, seek help.

You may be scared to admit weaknesses because it makes you look vulnerable. However, when I was young, neighbours helped each other and there was no shame involved. When my friend's mum was baking a cake and she needed some ingredients she would borrow from us. Nobody felt as though they were revealing their weaknesses. Neighbours were there to help each other.

To operate as a team you must be willing to

reveal your weaknesses. You must trust people in order to work with them. You must remove your mask. Instead of a non co-operative work style, you must develop co-operative work styles. The law of the jungle is survival of the fittest but the way of real success is the advancement of the neighbourhood, the community and the team. We don't want personal success. We want success for all of us.

> **Being honest about your weaknesses is a sign of inner strength.**

It is often people who are weak on the inside who put on the hardest face and look like the hardest nuts in town. To them, attacking is the best form of defence. However, the truly secure person is at home with his frailties. Frailties do not threaten this type of person. They know that they are still able to make their goals. They know that they don't have to be a superman to achieve their goals. In fact, there are no supermen or superwomen in this world.

> **The world is just full of normal people like you and me.**

Courage is deciding to go ahead despite your weaknesses. It is not denying that you have weaknesses. The courageous person is not the one who never experiences fear. He or she is the one who decided that fear would not stop them. These are the people who have left a positive legacy of a selfless life behind.

> **To work as a part of a team, you have to have inner security.**

If you are insecure, you will seek to dominate.

You will always be trying to prove to yourself and others your value. You will want to do everything because you are unsure of your personal value. You think that success demonstrates your value. An insecure person cannot be a successful team person. However, a person who has inner security is not threatened by the success of others. This kind of person can work as part of a team.

> **A secure person will listen to other people's ideas and implement those that are good advice.**

They don't care who thought of it. They evaluate an idea on its merits, not by whether they thought of it or someone else. It takes security to judge an idea on its merits. Insecurity leads to prejudice. Prejudice is anti-team. A prejudiced person cannot work in a team.

It is common for people to group together based on the similarities of the people involved. People who dress in a certain way group together; people of a certain income bracket, people who barrack for the same football team, or people of the same age group together.

In these groups we often get peer pressure. Peer pressure is not team play. It is a few insecure people dominating a group of similar looking people through intimidation. Peer pressure comes from insecure leaders and breeds defeated followers.

We need to group with people who are different from ourselves. This is the essence of a winning team. On a winning football team, they are not all centre forwards. Each player comes with his or her different skill. Their differences are meshed together to form a complete unit that can answer any attack of the opposition.

So don't let the difference of the other person

threaten you. Let their difference compliment you. Someone else's strength shouldn't make you feel weaker. We should realise what we can do together as a team.

> **A winning team employs the various skills of each participant who is secure in life.**

Even if you don't feel secure, you can choose to be. It only takes a decision.

> **We are not meant to be independent. The best word for success is interdependent.**

We become a community of people who have different skills and who choose to serve each other. We are whole people helping one another, not competing with each other.

Competition breeds the *'it's you or me'* syndrome. *'Either I get you, or you get me'*. That is not how it is supposed to be. That results in independent people, living in a neighbourhood, not trusting or caring to know each other.

When a nation faces a national calamity such as a war, people come together. They stop competing and start complementing. They have to, because if they don't they are going to lose the war. That is when the best comes out of people. Heroes come out of wars.

You don't need a war to be a hero. You can begin to live like that now. You don't need an emergency for you to live and work in a complementary framework and community. Don't look inwards on your own inadequacies. We all have them. Look outward to others. That is when you come alive. You realise your own potential when you release others instead of hindering the potential of others.

So don't think, '*I don't need my neighbour, I can do it myself*'. Think. '*I need my neighbour and my neighbour needs me*'. Someone once said, '*If you stand alone you will fall alone*'. Supermen and superwomen fall.

> ## Dictators fall, team workers thrive.

No one person has all the gifts, but a team of different personalities has all that is needed. Good teams succeed. Your success is my success. My success is your success.

Don't despise differences. Don't allow someone else's differences to make you insecure. Differences make you strong.

CHAPTER 23

What is your Framework?

$\mathcal{T}$o win in life, you have to have a framework.

> **A framework is a model
> from which you
> derive principles that help
> guide your decisions.**

Without a framework, there is no organisation in your life. Without a framework, you are drifting. You have no meaning, no absolutes and no right and wrong. You don't know if you have reached your destination because you don't know what your destination is.

You need to have the right framework. Success cannot be your only goal, because if it is and you achieve it you will be devastated. Success cannot be your only focus. You need a bigger focus than that. Everyone needs something bigger than himself or herself to live for. If we don't have that, then we live for ourselves and there will be no joy or achievement.

> **You need a framework and a purpose in life that is bigger than yourself.**

If success is your only goal then you can lose sight of moral values along the way. If you do this then you will not enjoy success when you have it.

Success cannot be your only goal. Success must be achieved within the context of more dominant values. There must be a *'trump card'* that is higher than what they call in business *'the bottom line'*. That is not the real bottom line. It might be in capitalism, but it is not when it comes to human values. Capitalism is good, but it must be regulated by man's moral oversight. There must be objective values, which to you are more important.

> **In your life there must be some principles that success respects.**

If you achieve success without the moral values that support it, then the success will destroy you. You will not have the self-discipline to make the right decisions for yourself and for your family.

Success alone is a poor teacher. Look at some of the well-known personalities that achieved success in the world's sense without a proper framework for life. What happens to them? You know what happened to them. Don't let that happen to your family.

You cannot tamper with absolutes and survive. You cannot cheat the *'system'*. Right is right whether you like it or not. Gravity is gravity; it doesn't matter what you call it.

Adultery is adultery. It is not success. It never will be success, no matter how the world may redefine it. It is a breach of trust. It is a destruction of relationships. It is a breakdown of the home, the only real security for children to grow up in a balanced and mature environment.

Dishonesty is dishonesty. It is not smart. If you cannot do something honestly then it is not worth doing at all. You need to have guidelines. You need to have a framework that will guide you safely.

Are you going to judge others by the standards of what many perceive success to be? What if someone is not rich? Can you respect them? What if someone is not beautiful, does not have a good figure, or doesn't wear the latest designer label? Are you going to determine someone's value by his or her income?

Is that what you are after in life? Is life in designer labels? Do people respect you because of what you wear or because of who you are?

Now it is good to wear nice clothes. I enjoy it. It is good to drive nice cars. I enjoy them. But these things are just things. You enjoy them, but they should not be your only focus.

You should gratefully enjoy good things. But in real success, you should share them with others. Don't let them rule you. That is success.

Do you rule money or does it rule you? Do you serve money or does money serve you? Money is a tool. It is supposed to serve us, so that we can decide what it will do and what good purposes can be achieved by it.

Money is one of our tools. Don't be afraid of it, use it. Don't hoard it. Do good with it.

When you succeed, you want to be able to enjoy that success. You don't want an *'easy come, easy go'* success. You don't want a success that brings with it jealousy, revenge, court cases, alcoholism, or children whose lives have been damaged by hurtful experiences.

The only way you can enjoy success is that when you go forward in life, make sure that success plays second fiddle to what you know is right.

You cannot change what is right. Just because it may help you get ahead, wrong doesn't suddenly become right.

> **There have to be guidelines in your life by which you can accurately judge your decisions.**

There have to be lines that you will not cross. Don't trust in your intelligence. Don't think, *'I am clever, I will know what to do. I will know how to get out of trouble'*.

The fact is that none of us is clever enough to negotiate our way through a minefield. Eventually, it is only a matter of time before we will put a foot wrong. Then lives that are ruined have to be stuck back together again. But sometimes you cannot find all the parts to stick back. Sometimes it is too late.

You have to draw lines in the sand and say, *'I will not cross these lines'*. That way you will be safe in your success.

When success comes you will enjoy it. It may not be as quick, but you will enjoy it. You will have success without regret. That is what success really is.

> **Success is the ability to enjoy your achievements without regret.**

CHAPTER 24

Just Keep Going

*J*t doesn't matter how things look now, just keep going. Things can change. As they say in politics, *'A day is a long time in politics'*. Things can change.

If you have one thing on your side, it is usually another chance.

> **No matter how things are
> at the moment,
> you have another chance.**

You are not out yet. Things may not have been going well, but when you look at it properly, you will realise that you are not out yet. You have another chance.

The thing I like about the morning is its freshness. The dew is on the grass, the air is still and you realise it is the dawning of a new day. A new day brings a new slate. It is an opportunity to have a brand new start in life. It is an opportunity to say, *'Other people have made mistakes also. I am going to put the past behind me. I am going to make new plans. I am going to start again'*.

Just keep going. Don't stop and think about how you are going to make it. You are going to make it. How are you going to make it? By keeping on going. So long as you keep going you are going to make it.

I like watching some of the world's best tennis players. Some of them have been down and at times it has looked like they are going to lose an important match. Yet the best of them are fighters. They just don't give up. They fight back.

> ## We all go down,
> ## but champions fight back.

It must feel tough in times like that. It would be easier just to get up and walk off. But the best don't walk off. They stay in there. The night might seem long, but they wait until the morning. The morning will come and they will get a fresh start. Every day is a chance for a fresh start. Every point in tennis is a chance for a new start. It can change. It is never too late for a change.

> ## One thing
> ## you notice about
> ## champions
> ## is their constancy.

When you look at some of the best tennis players, they have an ability to just get on with the job. No matter what has happened, they have an ability to put it out of their mind completely and to just get on with the next point. That is the stuff of champions.

> **Champions put
> everything out of their
> mind and get on
> with 'the next point'.**

They take it point at a time. They fight. They never give up. The only thing you must never do is give up.

A champion's face doesn't change, whether they are winning or losing. Whether they have played a master shot or played a huge miss. Their face is the same. The only thing they are concerned about is the next shot. The best player is just marching off to position him or herself for the next shot.

They don't dawdle off to the next point as though they were somehow still attached to their past. They are on with it. They walk off to the next point with purpose. They always have a purpose. Their purpose is the next point.

You might be half way towards fulfilling your goals. Don't stop there. Concentrate on finishing it. Concentrate. Keep going. Keep focused. Whether people are applauding or not does not matter. Whether people recognise you are on the court or not doesn't matter. Just play the game.

> **Concentrate and play to win.**

There are times that you do not know what to do next. You do not know how you are going to get through. You can't see a way out of the problem. That is the time to just keep going.

You don't always have the answers. You don't always have the plan. There are no super planners who always know what to do. Sometimes you just don't know what to do.

> ## You don't have to have the answers before you keep going.

What you do then is just keep going. You may not know what to do. You don't have to know what to do. It will work out. Things change. Don't stop. Just keep going.

You can't get an idea sitting down. When you are moving, it will come to you. Just keep moving.

> ## Champions keep moving, even when it looks like they are overwhelmed.

The rule is – when you don't know how you are going to get out of something, just keep moving forward. Sometimes it is not your concern how success will come. Sometimes it is not up to you. Your job is just to make sure at those times that you don't stall. That is all you have to do.

Success will come. Will you still be on the road when it does, or will you have packed your bags and gone home?

Once when we were building, I had a large debt and all the money I borrowed had run out. We could not pay our workers, had purchased large amounts of building materials on credit and had only three weeks left in which we had to finish the job.

I didn't know what to do. I wanted to stay in bed. But I had to go and face the workers and greet them, *'Good morning'*. That was hard to say, but I said it. All I had to do that morning was to go to work and face it. I had no idea what to do, but all I had to do was to go.

Later that day I had an idea. That idea was a long shot. In fact, it was a very long shot. But it worked. People stood with me and it worked. We paid off all our debts and all our loans and finished the building in seven weeks, without owing a dollar on it. We got through. It was hard, but we just kept going.

One meaning of patience is that you keep doing what you know is right. Self-control means that you do what you know is right. Patience means that you just keep doing it.

> **So in order to be stable you need knowledge first, self-control second and patience third.**

One without the other is not enough. Sometimes you have to change. Sometimes you don't.

> **When you are doing what is right and it is not working, you don't change – you just keep doing it.**

Just keep doing it. It will work. It may not be as quick as you hoped, but it will work. Your children may not be showing the fruit you hoped for so quickly. Don't give up. Keep directing them. Don't abandon your responsibilities towards your children.

Keep at it. The fruit will come – if you don't give up.

CHAPTER 25

Thinking

*W*hen you win, when you get there, be thankful. Don't say, *'I did it myself and I deserve what I have'*. The spirit with which you win is important. Don't win with pride. Win with grace. He or she who wins with pride is bitter and harsh towards others. They say, *'I won by myself, I did it myself. What is your excuse? I am not going to help you. It is your fault if you are not winning. I don't have time for people like you'*.

> **When you win, look around and help others.**

Look around and see who is in need of help, the way you once were. Don't blame them for their current state, but think of ways in which you can get through to them and help them – one more time.

> **Think in terms of grace,
> not in terms of harsh judgement.**

You can win in two different ways. You can win by yourself and believe you are self-made or you can win with grace. The former person becomes hard and unforgiving. The latter person bears fruit and is a source of encouragement to others – right to their last days. Their sense of grace grows increasingly as they age.

Remember that you are not self-made. Others helped you. Your parents raised you, despite their mistakes. They did a lot of good for you. They worked late at night to get you through. Maybe you didn't understand each other well, but they tried their best.

Others helped you. When you look back over your life, you remember many people who were there when you needed them. There are people who spoke into your life when you needed it. They were examples from whom you were able to learn from and follow. Remember that you are not self-made.

Raise your expectations. You will perform at the level that you expect yourself to perform at. It may take you a while to reach that level. Expect to reach a higher level than the one you are currently at.

> **Raise your expectations and you will ultimately lift your standard.**

You will hit your target. You have to lift your target and practice until you hit it. Then raise it again and practice until you hit it again.

You raise your expectations by raising the standard of your thinking. The way you think is critical. This is where people begin to lower or begin to raise their game.

> **It may take a while, but your raised standard will eventually match your raised thinking.**

So raise the standard of your thinking. You cannot rise above the level that you think. If you think you are not good enough, eventually you will lower your standard. You will stop trying. You will start to get sluggish. Your activity will match the way you think.

However, if you raise the level of your thinking then your results will eventually reach that level. This is very important. It will not change your life overnight. Neither can you plant a seed and get fruit from a tree overnight. However, change will come.

**Fruit takes time.
It is the result of cultivated habits.**

One of the most important habits you can cultivate is the habit of good thinking. Your speech will follow your thinking. What other people think of you will always be determined by what you think of yourself. Don't blame others for how they think of you. They are only following your own example. Change the way you think of yourself.

Think that you can do it. Think it long enough until you discover the things in your life that will need to change for you to reach your expectations.

Thinking is a very important start. It is something that you never relax on, the rest of your life. But it is not enough. In scientific terms, *'it is necessary, but not sufficient'*.

When you start to think the right way, eventually you will start to understand where you have been falling down. You will start to understand where you have been going wrong, where your guard has been down and where you have been slack and negligent.

This is the crucial point. When these things dawn on your understanding, what you do about it is the critical issue. This is where you make it or break it. This is the point that correct thinking is supposed to bring you to.

If you turn back at this point, all the books about positive thinking will not help you.

> **It is not the thinking
> that matters
> at the end of the day;
> it is the doing
> that counts.**

It is the action you take to change these areas that will determine whether your life changes. It is not what is left to you in a will or what the government can do for you that will change your life.

> **The way you think
> determines the
> amount of strength
> that you have.**

When your thinking is right, your body eventually comes in line with your thoughts and you find the strength that you need.

You will start to rule over your body, to a certain extent, by the way you think. Some people are sick all the time. Sometimes, though not all the time, this is because of the way they think. That is how they see themselves.

When your thinking becomes encouraged, you will find the strength that you need to do the job and more.

The way you think about your marriage will determine the happiness you have there.

Think and speak right in your household.
Build your marriage and children
with the words of your mouth.

Think and speak right in your business. Tell your associates that they can do it. Let others know that they can do great things and that they too can be a crocodile in a lizard's world.

About the Author

Kent Hodge lives with his wife Ruth and five children on the outskirts of London in the United Kingdom. Kent travels extensively in Africa and other nations, as an educator and administrator. For more than 15 years Kent and Ruth have shared the work in Nigeria of training over 7,000 leaders for the African continent. This has given them experience in leadership, education, building, conference speaking and in raising scholarship funding around the world for the college's current average enrolment of 1,600 students.